NEO ANTHROPOLOGICAL THEORY

About the Author

Gaya Pandey (*b.* 1954) is one of Senior faculties of the University Department of Anthropology, Ranchi University, Ranchi (Jharkhand). After passing M.Sc. Examination of Anthropology from Ranchi University with first division in 1979, he joined at A.N. Sinha Institute of Social Studies, Patna as a Doctoral Research Fellow of University Grants Commission, Government of India for his doctoral Research and Ph.D. degree. He was awarded Ph.D. degree by Ranchi University in 1984 and get honour to join UGC Centre of Advance Study. Department of Anthropology Ranchi University, Ranchi in February 1985 and since than he is serving in the department. During his 36 years of teaching and research experiences, he has contributed two and half dozen research articles in Journal of National and International repute and edited books. He has to his credit the publication of 21 books in different branches of anthropology. Most of his books are textbooks written in English and Hindi languages. Through book writing he has touched almost all major branches of anthropology. Besides reading and writing he is also recognised Ashu Kavi (extempore Poet). Some of his recently published books are Manavashastriya Anusandhan Vidhi Ewam Taknik, Bhartiya Manavashastra, Jatil Samaj ka Manavshastra, Bhartiya Janajatiya Sanskriti, Developmental authropology, Bio-cultural Evolution, Jaivik Sanskritik Udvikas, Bhartiya Pragaitihasik Puratattrik Manavshastra, Sampreshnatmak Manavshastria communicational anthropology. The book Chikitsatmak Manavshastra (Medical Anthropology), Social-cultural anthropology and Neo Anthropoligical Theory are under press.

NEO ANTHROPOLOGICAL THEORY

Gaya Pandey

CONCEPT PUBLISHING COMPANY PVT. LTD.
NEW DELHI-110059

ISBN-13: 978-93-5125-226-9 (HB)
ISBN-13: 978-93-5125-227-6 (PB)

First Published : 2017

Published and Printed by

Concept Since 1974

Concept Publishing Company Pvt. Ltd.
Regd. Office:
A/15-16, Commercial Block, Mohan Garden,
New Delhi-110059 (INDIA)
Phones : 25351460, 25351794, *Fax* : 091-11-25357109
Email : publishing@conceptpub.com
Website: www.conceptpub.com

Editorial Office: H-13, Bali Nagar, New Delhi-110 015, India.

Cataloging in Publication Data—DK Courtesy: D.K. Agencies (P) Ltd. <docinfo@dkagencies.com>

Pandey, Gaya, 1954- **author.**
Neo anthropological theory / Gaya Pandey.
pages cm
Includes bibliographical references and index.
ISBN 9789351252269

1. Anthropology. I. Title.

DDC 301 23

Dedicated To

Dedicated to mother Smt. Ansuiya Devi, wife Smt. Indu Devi, daughters—Sudha, Suman, Sarita and Anu, Son—Shekhar, daughter-in-law Sullavi, and grandsons—Kushagra and Harshit with all regards, respects and love who have been always behind me as a force to accomplish the task of book writing successfully by extending their all kinds of support in caring for my poor health condition.

Preface

The book entitled, "Neo Anthropological Theory" deals with only those theories which have been propounded by anthropological thinkers after Second World War, particularly from the middle of twentieth century. Neo anthropological theories and thinkers are taught as a special paper in postgraduate and undergraduate departments of anthropology in different universities of our country. About classical anthropological theory we have a number of books, but on neo anthropological theory, we have only few books. As a result students have to face difficulty in the study of neo anthropological theory. Keeping in view problems of students, this book has been written systematically in simple English language. So, purpose of book is purely contextual written with the view to help the students.

The book writing has been in existence since the birth of civilization, but the purpose behind the composition of the book differs from one contribution to another. The author does not claim to have contributed something new which cannot be found in the writing of the others. Sometimes others' expressions have been followed word by word in toto. All these have been done with the sole aim to bring maximum materials under one cover for the benefits of the students. The simple language of the book will definitely help students to understand the contributions of great masters of neo anthropological theory.

One cannot claim to be perfect in expression. The best reviewer of the book are readers. The readers are requested to make the author aware of the weaknesses and mistakes of the book, so that, its quality could be improved in future. If readers are satisfied with the materials and presentation of the book, it will be a great success for the author.

The book has been written with the support of works of great masters of anthropology, teachers, collegues, research scholars and students of anthropology department, family members and the team of Concept Publishing Company Pvt. Ltd., New Delhi. Now, it is my sacred duty to extend gratitude and thanks to all of them individually and collective. I extend my sincere gratitude to all great masters and authors of anthropological thoughts, whose contributions have played great role directly and indirectly in completion of the book. I also extend thanks to all teachers of the department who encouraged me much for completing the book. All research scholars and students of the department deserve thanks for their encouragement in completion of book. I extend thank to all family members who have taken every care of me.

In completion of the book, I am thankful to Shri Ashok Kumar Mittal and his team for publishing the manuscript with meticulous care.

Mahalaya
13th October, 2015

Gaya Pandey
Department of Anthropology,
Ranchi University, Ranchi,
Jharkhand

Contents

Introduction

Before Second World War anthropologists were able to formulate the theories of evolution, diffusion, function, structure-function and culture and personality. The scholars associated with these theories were Morgan, Tylor, Maine, McLennan, Bachofen, Bastian, Ratzel, Graebner, Schmidt, Wissler, Kroeber, Franz Boas, Malinowaski Radcliffe-Brown, Margret Mead, Ruth Benedict Linton and Cora du-Bois. These theories propounded by these scholars are now, known as classical theories. It is because neo anthropological theories have emerged in place of old anthropological theories. The establishment of neo anthropological theory began in Post-Second World War period around middle of twentieth century. Thus, all anthropological theories which were established before the Second World War beginning from evolutionary and ending into culture and personality are now term as old anthropological theories. Anthropological theories which were developed in Post-Second World War period around 1950 and onwards are known as neo anthropological theories today.

It is also worth mentioning here that neo anthropological theories have followed two paths based on two different principles. These two different paths and principles are materialist and idealist. According to materialist principle the aim of anthropological study is to find out basic law that governs the development of society and culture. The materialists treat anthropology as an empirical science. They try to apply objective and scientific methodology for the study of society and culture. They are of opinion that the proper research strategy in a given time can yield basic law of social-cultural development. This basic law can be compared to the basic law of natural sciences. The early scholars belonging to this line of anthropological theories were Morgan, Tylor, Frazer, Maine, McLennan, Bachofen, Bastian, Spencer and others. The school of evolution was basically related to scientific study of society and culture. The present day scholars associated with the study of cultural ecology, Ecological anthropology and cultural materialism are supporter of materialist view point of society and culture.

The another principle idealists consider culture essentially a mental or psychological phenomenon. They do not accept the existence of natural law in the development of society and culture. According to idealists the aim of anthropology is not to search a universal law. Rather the aim of anthropology is to describe social and cultural phenomena in detail. They are of opinion that anthropology is a branch of humanities. Like humanities, detailed and accurate description are sufficient. The followers of this anthropological thought were Franz Boas and his pupils. The scholars of this anthropological throught were of view that each culture is unique and product of its own cultural and historical circumstances. Their concept of cultural relativism and historical particularism precluded the possibility of cross-cultural comparison and universal generalization. The school of culture and personality was also similar. Now-a-days the scholars associated with the theories of Ethno-science, cognitive anthropology, structural anthropology, symbolic anthropology, Interpretive anthropology, Phenomenological anthropology, Political economy and post-modernism belong to idealists group.

Some other thinkers are of opinion that there should be synthesis of objectivity and subjectivity. The functionalists and structuralists held a mid path by accepting both the principles and finding out a mid way to study society and culture. Malinowski, who laid the foundation of functional school in anthropology was of opinion that culture is an instrument for the satisfaction of needs of human individuals. He emphasized upon the bio-psychic needs of human individuals and propounded the functional theory. According to him main function of culture has been to keep the existence of human individuals by satisfying their bio-psychic needs. He divided bio-psychic needs into three categories—primary, secondary and tertiary and for each categories there were cultural responses. The functional theory of culture provided a universal character of culture and society.

The structural functionalists, under the leadership of A.R. Radcliffe Brown, treated culture and society as an abstract concept which could not be observed. They developed the concept of social structure—the principles that organise persons in society or group. According to them social structure was the only worthy topic for study of culture and society. It was because the actual roles and relationships of persons in group can be observed.

Radcliffe Brown was influenced by Herbert Spencer. Like Spencer he believed that the ultimate aim of anthropology was to search for a universal law. Both functional and structural functional schools had ignored history completely. They had concentrated on contemporary societies. They treated society and culture as static and timeless. They did not take into account changes in society and culture and did not provide any causal explanation.

In Post-Second World War specialists of several sub-fields of anthropology such as biological, prehistoric, archaeological, social-cultural and linguistic anthropology evaluated their methodologies critically. Attempts were made to create new approaches. W. Taylor (1948) emphasised upon the foundation of new prehistoric archaeology. S.Washburn laid emphasis on the foundation of new Biological anthropology. Social-cultural anthropologists adopted techniques and methods of linguistics. As a result new ethnography or ethno science came into existence. Linguistic anthropology also sharpened its techniques, methods and approaches and sought new directions.

By mid-twentieth century a movement arose in cultural anthropology. This movement was dedicated to the improvement of standards of ethnographic description and analysis within cultural anthropology. This movement emphasised upon the use of techniques of linguistics as its source and inspiration. This movement was given the name as New Ethnography or Ethno science. The movement originated at Yale University in USA, but gradually spread throughout the United States of America under such names as Ethno-linguistics, Ethno-science, Ethno-semantics or New Ethnography. This movement was associated with highly operationalised paradigmatic rendering of cultural phenomena. Here cultural phenomena have come to be associated with linguists description of phonology and grammar.

All these efforts led to a closer cooperation in four fields of anthropology, biological anthropology, prehistoric anthropology, social-cultural anthropology and linguistic anthropology.

The New Prehistoric archaeological anthropology viewed their findings as representative of cultural system. They attempted to grasp the meaning of Prehistoric archaeological remains, not as an end in themselves, but as a means to understanding human beings who had made them and the societies in which they had lived.

The New Biological anthropology projected human evolution in the background of culture and ecology. The field studies of living primates searched for inter-relationships between animal and human social behaviour.

Many present day linguists concerned themselves with cultural and psychological elements of language. The cultural anthropologists adopted linguistic methodology as a model of their own studies.

Thus, anthropological efforts to revise and refine older concepts followed many different directions. But over all concern was the attempt to discover units of explanation that can be used cross-culturally in an objective and unbiased manner. Dissatisfied with historical particularism, the anthropologists began to feel that meaningful cross-cultural comparisons could not rest upon undefined categories used earlier such as trait, complex, pattern, theme, custom, folkways and so on.

The interest in cross-cultural analysis attracted the scholars towards the attempt to discover universal in culture. They realised that human behaviour was flexible and culture also varied. But inspite of variation culture had some common ground of existence. These developments were not unrelated to bring the study of primitive societies in to greater relationship with complex one. For long period anthropologists has treated primitive cultures as timeless and unchanging isolates. But such a romantic outlook could no longer be maintained. Changes occurring in the world after Second World War touched primitives, peasants, towns men and industrialized city dwellers. In order to study such changes the concept of acculturation was adopted. The study of change began in anthropology. The study of acculturation began to investigate as to how primitives became member of modern society, how peasants became industrialised farmers and how migrants adjust to new environment.

The community study method was perhaps the first conscious attempt to extend the insights gained from the study of homogenous societies to more complex ones. The community study method was a departure from the study of particular tribal groups. It demonstrated that cultures were functionally dependent parts of larger wholes. But this method contained no direction as to how various larger wholes could be brought into relationship with each other into a meaningful way.

Searching for a wider framework in which finding of prehistoric archaeological anthropology, Biological anthropology, social-cultural anthropology and linguistic anthropology could be filled, anthropologists rediscovered evolution, known as neo evolutionary theory.

From the mid 1950 till now, neo anthropological theories have taken the following shapes:

- Neo evolutionary anthropological theory
- Structural anthropological theory
- New psychological anthropological theory
- Biologised anthropological theory
- Cognitive anthropology
- Symbolic anthropological theory
- Interpretive anthropological theory
- Phenomenological anthropological theory
- Critical anthropological theory (Political Economy)
- Modernism theory
- Post-modernism theory
- Industrialism and post-industrialism
- Globalisation theory
- Legacy of Karl Marx in Anthropology
- Legacy of Max Weber in Anthropology

Now, it will be worth presenting here the details of each anthropological theories one by one.

1
Neo Evolutionary Theory

Introduction

In anthropology theory of evolutionism was pronounded by pioneers like E.B. Tylor, H.J.S. Maine, J.F. McLennan and James Frazer Britain, J.J. Bachofen and Adolf Bastian in Germany and L.H. Morgan in America from the beginning of 1850 to 1890. These nineteenth century evolutionists held in common that culture had progressed in unilineal sequence from simple to complex form. Such progress in cultural evolution of mankind was witnessed all over the world. This principle of early evolutionists was known as cultural parallelism. Its was the concept of psychic unity of mankind which had played significant role in evolutionary reconstruction of nineteenth century evolution. These scholars had used deductive approach while presenting the historical reconstruction of culture. They had developed the concept of survivals which had played role in comparative method and representing the early stages of culture.

The evolutionary theory of nineteenth century evolutionists was criticised by a number of scholars who propounded their own theories including their own counterparts known as neo evolutionists. The neo evolutionists considered all criticisms of diffusionists, functionalists, structural-factionalists and their own criticism and attempted to revise or revive the evolutionary theory in such a way which was acceptable to all and applicable in all branches of anthropology. The nineteenth century evolutionists were labelled as classical evolutionists. The rediscovered form or revived form of evolutionary theory is known as Neo evolutionary theory and scholars associated with this theory are known as neo evolutionists.

The supporters of Neo Evolutionary Theory are as follows:

- Leslie A. White
- Betty Megers
- Julian H. Steward
- Lewis Binford
- V. Gordon Childe
- Marshal Shahlins
- Elman Service

Of above mentioned scholars, all were from America except V. Gordon Childe who belonged to Britain. These twentieth century scholars had revived and reformulated the classical cultural evolutionism.

During the era of Franz Boas, historical particularism and cultural relativisms flourished. Both historical particularism and cultural relativism had prohibited the possibility of cross-cultural comparisons and universal generalisations. But after his death, i.e., in Post-Boasian era, the influence of historical particularism and cultural relativism went out of scene and crowded picture of anthropological theory emerged. One of new elements in this crowded pictures was nomothetic anthropology, which was suppressed by Franz Boas's preference for ideographic anthropology. In contrast to ideographic anthropology, nomothetic anthropology emphasised upon cross-cultural comparisions and universal generalisations.

The search for cross-cultural generalisations was introduced by Human Relation Area File, established in 1940s by George Peter Moodock at Yale University. It was used by Whiting and Child in 1950, for research purposes. The outstanding new nomothetic theory was neo evolutionism that was anti-Boasian in some ways.

LESLIE A. WHITE (1900-1975)

In America theory of neo cultural evolutionism was propounded by Leslie A. White. He had achieved his anthropological training under the guidance of Franz Boas, the builder of American anthropology. He had obtained a strong Boasian outlook at his graduate studies. At the New School in New York he was taught by Alexender A. Golden

Wieser. At the University of Chicago he was influenced by Boasians from where he had obtained Ph.D. degree in 1927. In the year 1925 his first article was published which was full of Boasian plea for the importance of cultural factors in the determination of personality. This was parallel to the programme upon which Margret Mead was about to work.

White had got a chance to teach at the University of Buffalo for two years. This University was situated in the territory of Iroquois. Here, he got a chance to study the contributions of L.H. Morgan. After reading Morgan's contribution, White developed anti-Boasian position. He was surprised to read as to why Morgan was forgotten. He was shocked at those who had accepted Morgan as worthless example of speculative philosophy on the basis of second hand opinion. He accepted Morgan as a remarkable scholar. Through Morgan he also got interest in Marx and Engeles. By 1929, he was deeply involved in Marxist matter and got a chance to visit Soviet Union. He returned from Soviet Union to take the position of teaching at the University of Michigan. He succeeded in establishing Michigan as one of major centres of anthropology. He was hostile towards historical particularism, cultural relativism, psychological reductionism, doctrine of free will theological teleology.

White's views regarding neo evolutionary theory can be summarised into his two books:

- The Science of Culture (1949)
- The Evolution of Culture (1959)

The book *Science of Culture* is collection of essays. But his book, *The Evolution of Culture* is an exposition of course and process of evolution. In this book White has considered culture as a system of its own kind, suigeneris. It was similar to Kroeber's concept of super organic. According to him, cultural laws would constitute the science of culturology Leslie White had given the name cultrology for nomothetic study of culture. The axis point of this system culturology was thermodynamics. Thermodynamics deals with conversion of forms of energy in the universe. White was impressed with second law of thermodynamics. According to the second law of thermodynamics universe is running down structurally and dynamically resulting in increased entropy or disorder.

According to White biological evolution works in opposite direction taking negative entropy from the universe and increasing order in the production of complex forms of life. Cultural evolution which Supplants biological evolution in case of Homosapiens and ancestral species, enhances this trend.

To explain the evolution of culture, White proposed a Thermodynamic law. According to this law culture evolves as energy harnessed per capita per year is increased or as the efficiency means of putting this energy to work is increased. He formulated his cultural evolution law as follows:

$$C = E \times T$$

Where C = Culture
T = Technology
E = Energy

White defined four major stages of cultural evolution. Each stage had come into existence as a result of energy revolution. These four stages were as follows:

- Tool invention revolution
- Neolithic revolution
- Fuel revolution of eighteenth century
- Atomic revolution of twentieth century

The first revolution was invention of tools which increased the ability of human body to obtain food calorie.

The second revolution was neolithic revolution, a termed coined by archeologist V. Gordon Childe to describe the increased control over food energy achieved by domestication of animals and plants.

The third revolution was fuel revolution which gave rise to technology for controlling them and utilising them for works.

The forth revolution was atomic revolution in which technologies were developed to control atomic energy for utilising them in works.

In between these revolutions culture evolved as technology for using these new energy sources improved.

According to White energy is more important than technology. It is because efficiency of technology depends upon energy. Technology is vehicles means and select on, whereas energy is the dynamic living force that animates cultural system and develops them to higher levels and forms.

The operation of this law is potent in the history of mankind. Hunting and gathering subsistence produced a some low level of usable energy in the portion to the amount expanded by hunters. Neither fire nor wind were source of energy in the earliest and longest stage of cultural evolution.

The energy captured was limited to what man's own muscle could provide as means. White estimated that in hunting and gathering societies the amount of energy captured was limited to about 1/20 horse power per capita per year.

As soon as plants and animals were domesticated a Quantum Jump in cultural evolution took place. Now man could control his sources of energy. This meant a greater yields in usable energy with less energy expenditure by man. This was agricultural revolution as a result of which labour specialization, large population, even-more sophisticated technology in short civilization like Mesopotamia, Egypt, Greece and Rome came into existence.

Energy exploitation by capture then hit the plateau area forced by monosophistic controls by elite, until the fuel revolution took place. This corresponded to growth of industrial production which used coal as a major source of energy. It was much greater than the potential of farming and herding. The amount of energy per capita per year went another quantum jump upward. But this time development was more spectacular than agriculture.

Forced by war and search for larger shares of economic market, men developed their industrial technology to the point at which they could not continue the full productions profitably in their factories. Now, another breakthrough in the harnessing of energy, the atomic revolution took place. In this way White's evolutionary stages were savagery, barbarism civilisation and energy revolution.

An integral part of White's thermodynamic system was layer cake model of culture. His layer cake model of culture places technology and economy at the bottom, ideology at the top and social and political organization in the middle.

In the determination of cultural evolution, the bottom layer predominated because innovations in technology and energy took place there. In assigning priority to technology and economy over ideology as the impetus for cultural changes, White was a cultural materialist. He had obtained materialism from Marxism, Morgan and Friedrich Engels. White was so impressed by Morgan that he decided to rehabilitate Morgan as a cultural evolutionist. His criticism of Boas was even stronger than Derek Freeman's criticism of Margaret Mead.

JULIAN H. STEWARD (1902-1972)

Julian H. Steward is regarded as founder of modern cultural ecology and Ecological anthropology. Steward was also Boasian by intellectual tradition and upbringing. He was a long time professor at the university of Illinois. At the University of Illinois, he got opportunity to train a host of distinguished political and economic anthropologists. Such was Morton, Fried, Andrew Vayda, Eric Wolf and Elman Service. Under the able guidance and intellectual leadership of Steward, the modern concept of cultural ecology emerged. The modern concept of cultural ecology nurtured a nomothetic approach to anthropology. It is because it focused on the articulation between culture and nature. In this way anthropology was linked to nomothetic natural sciences like biology, demography and chemistry.

His famous book, '*Theory of Culture Change*' was published in 1955 from the University of Illinois Press, Urbana. Steward's work grew out of 'Culture area' concept used by Boasian, A.L. Kroeber and O Clark Wissler to demonstrate the American Indian groups. Each group inhabited a geographical area to which it adopted through its culture. In this way cultural adoption of geographical area takes place. The adaptation became the main theme of cultural ecology. In cultural ecology adaptation means the result of culture adjusting to environment.

In 1936, Steward published a seminal paper on economic and social basis of bands. In this essay he distinguished bands from tribe chiefdom and state. He define three types of bands:

- Patrilineal band
- Matrilineal band
- Composite band

Steward linked each type of band to particular ecological circumstances. Steward's cultural ecological approach, attracted some Boasian to rethink their electical approach to anthropological explanation and concentrate instead on cultural biology. Electical approach is such an approach in which anthropologists are sometimes cultural materialists and other time cultural idealists. As a result a reinterpretation of some famous anthropological events like North-west coast ceremony of Potlatch took place. This ceremony according to Ruth Benedict was a wasteful drive for social status. But cultural ecologists like Helen Codere and Wayne. He Suttles later on explained this custom of Potlatch as an ecologically adaptive redistributive feast.

As a cultural ecologist, steward was not a cultural evolutionist. He had taken interest in evolutionism to find out White's pronouncement extreme. He distanced himself from White by calling White's brand of evolutionism as universal evolutionism and his own brand as multilineal or multilinear evolutionism. He called nineteen century brand as unilineal evolutionism. In this way, he associated himself with multilinear brand of evolutionism. Steward's view implied by these labels was that he was specialist and White was generalist. According to him the label unilineal meant that culture had progressed in unilineal directions and could not skip stages. But as a multilineal evolutionist Steward believed that evolution could branch off in many directions as cultures could adapt to varied circumstances.

MARSHAL SAHLINS AND ELMAN SERVICE

Marshal Sahlins and Elman Service were colleagues at the University of Michigan. At the University of Michigan they had worked in close association with White. As a students of Steward, Service maintained his interest in the ecological basis of social groupings. This was the theoretical frame work for his popular text '*Primitive Social Organization*' (1962):

Sahlins began his work in economic anthropology. He was a strong proponent of cultural evolutionism and cultural materialism before he began to combine French Structural and historical analyses in the late 1960s.

In 1960, Sahlins and Service co-authored their book, '*Evolution and Culture*'. In this book they attempted to reconcile the views of Steward and White. In the time honourned anthropological tradition of treating biology and culture as analogues, they made argument that like biological evolution, cultural evolution also had two differently directions. The direction of general evolution was pursued by White and the direction of particular evolution was persued by Steward. White was concerned with long term evolutionary progress and Steward was concerned with local special adaptation similar to natural selection. Thus, with the help of Sahlins and Service, the controversy of General evolution and special or particular evolution was solved. They propagated the view that White and Steward were not antagonistic, rather they were complementary to each other.

Sahlins and Service worked at Michigan University together for a decade. Along with White they formed a powerful evolutionary triumvirate. They established Michigan school of anthropology. This school influenced a number of other cultural evolutionists and cultural ecologists such as Alexander Allands Jr. Robert Carneiro and Yehudi Cohen. They kept the nomothetic approach of cultural anthropology alive.

BETTY MEGGERS

Archaeologist Betty Meggers was a student of White. She was very much inspired by White's Thermodynamic formula for cultural evolution, i.e., $C = E \times T$.

The cultural evolutionism had a major impact on prehistoric archaeology mainly through White. The prehistoric archaeology since its establishment in the mid nineteenth century had progressed through several stages linked to the stages in development of cultural anthropology. There were functionalist archaeology, Marxist archaeology and culture-historic archaeology. Pro-Functionalist archaeology was conjunction of archaeology with functionalism. Marxist archaeology was conjunction of archaeology with Marxism. The culture historic archaeology was archaeology in the era of Boasian historical particularism. This archaeology was represented by mid-Western taxonomic methods. This method of archaeological classification was used in culture historical archaeology. But Betty

Meggers found the culture historical approach unproductive. She decided to apply the White's formula, C = E × T to archaeology. She believed that if archaeologist knew Technology (T) and Environment (E) they could reconstruct Culture (C). This idea of Betty Meggers was developed further by an another student of White, Lewis Binford.

LEWIS BINFORD

Lewis Binford was a student of Leslie A .White. Being influenced by nomothetic anthropology of White, he also attempted to understand archaeology from the point of view of layer-cake model of White. With this approach he became leader of new archaeology of 1960s. The new archaeology is nomothetic archaeology advanced by Binford and others. It is also known as Processual archaeology.

Binford was trained in cultural historical archaeology of Franz Boas, but he changed his idea when he came in contact with White. He became the founder of nomothetic archaeology later on. According to him archaeology is an integral part of anthropology. It is because archaeologists and anthropologists share the same goal to explain the similarities and differences among cultures. The meaning to explain is to offer generalizations about cultural system and cultural evolution. He was of opinion that cultures change in both natural environment and other cultures. But in explaining change some part of cultures are more important than others. He rejected the conception of culture as "shared value". This conception was propounded by Benedict, a scholar of culture personality school and student of Franz Boas. Clyde Klukhohn was also a supporter of this conception for whom culture was ethods, spiritual character. Binford had adopted White's layer-cake models of culture. According to him artifacts in archaeology are object of material culture. Artitacts can reflect all three layers which yield a well balanced pictures of cultures in the past. For their purpose the archaeologists should be trained as ethnologists, so that, they can learn how artifacts function in present and then 'read' these functions in past. Under the leadership of Binfood the new archaeology revived the nineteenth century 'comparative method'.

Binford had developed a number of nomothetic devices to make archaeology scientific. His one device was hypothetico deductive model for scientific explantion. It was a philosophical model for scientific explanation which was used by Binford in new archaeology. This model directed scientists to hypothesize "covering laws" from which specific circumstances could be deducted, predicted or retrodicted. And then compared with present reality. His another device was general system theory. It was a cybernetic model of culture used in new archaeology. It involved "feedback loops" and "positive" or system maintaining and "negative" or system changing, cause and effect change.

Binford was vigorously against the psychological explanation of culture. Like White and Kroeber, Binford had opposed the great man theory of history. He was of opinion that human behaviours were determined by forces-laws of which individuals were largely unaware and over which they could exert little control.

Hyper Scientific, antihumanistic and positivist attitude made cultural evolutionism and new archaeology pills to bitter for many anthropologists to swallow. But because of its preoccupation with cultural process the New archaeology was called as processual archaeology. Beginning in 1980s, Processual archaeology attracted Severe criticism from post-processualists. According to post-processualists, processual archaeology possessed every thing that was wrong with modern science. At the same time in cultural anthropology post-modernists severely criticised modern science for many of the same reason.

V. GORDON CHILDE (1892-1957)

V. Gordon Childe was an archaeologist by profession in Britain. He made comparison between archaeological remains of East and Europe. On the basis of comparisons between archaeological remains of East and Europe, he revived the theory of cultural evolution. He occupied the position of a neo evolutionist. His major contributions were as follows:

1925: The Down of Western Civilisation
1934: Light on most Ancient East

1946: What happened in history
1951: Social Evolution
1951: Man makes himself
1953: What is history

Childe had attempted to revive the theory of evolution in his book '*Social Evolution*' (1951). The nineteenth centuary evolutionists were criticised as armchair anthropolgists. They were also criticised for their deductive approach. Being archaeologist, he made a comparisions between facts gathered from East and Europe. On the basis of his factual analysis of artifacts, he brought in to light the concept of social evolution.

He attempted to show that some major events had occured throughout the world. The chrnological study of those events reveal clearly that universal evolution of culture had taken place. Due to his such view the label universal evolutionist was attached to him. According to him universal evolution is concerned with four major revolution which had occurred in the world in chronological order. These revolutions were as follows:

- Agricultural Revolution
- Urban Revolution
- Industrial Revolution
- Knowledge Revolution

Agricultural revolution came into existence in Neolithic period. The period of this revolution has been far more than other revolutions. It started in neolithic period and is continuing even to day in one form or the other.

The Urban revolution started in Bronze Age nearly in 3000 B.C. in prehistoric towns. It assumed the form of religio-administrative centre in historic ages. A number of secular cities emerged for different purposes. Now, we have metropolises. This revolution is also going on in one form or the other.

The industrial revolution occured during seventeenth and eighteenth century in England and it gradually spread in all parts of the world. It is also going on in one form or the other.

Now-a-day, we are passing through fourth revolution known as knowledge revolution.

From the above chronological events which have occured in the world at universal level, it is quite clear that cultural evolution is a universal phenomenon. His universal stages of cultural evolution were accepted to all. Scholars gladly accept that in the beginning there was a stage of hunting gathering or foraging. This stage was replaced by agricultural stage when the food gatherers became food producers and wandering bands and cave dwellers became village dwellers; More and more production of food materials brought specialisation of labour and which gradually made man interdependent and town dwellers. After industrial revolution mankind became industrial city dwellers.

CULTURAL ECOLOGY

As referred to earlier that Julian H. Steward is regarded as founder of modern cultural Ecology who introduced nomothetic study in cultural ecology. Under cultural ecology, the study of interactions between environment and culture are made. It well known facts that culture makes adaptation with local environment. On the other hand environment also makes adaptation with culture. Thus, both makes adaptation with each other. In fact both influence each other. Both are not isolated. Rather they are interrelated, interdependent and maintaining their co-existence since time immemorial. The examination of these interactions are made under cultural ecology.

According to Steward, the world is divided into a number of geographical environments. For example hilly, plateae, forest, desert, coastal, island and plain. In different types of environment different types of soil, river, mountain, lake, fountain, flora, fauna, human races and other natural resources are found. In different environments different forms of culture are in existence. All material resources of an environment becomes associated with the culture of mankind who are found living there. House, food, technology, economy, marriage, family, religion and communication of the people revolve round the environment. Thus, each environment develops a special culture. Each culture develops technology and belief to cope with the environment. All natural objects find place in cultural system.

The societies with similar environment and technology also show similarity in their social and political organisation. Under cultural ecology Steward had attempted to study interactions between man and their habitat. It is the important task of cultural ecology to find out the interaction between man and habitat. According to Steward, the four process of cultural ecology are as follows:

- **Secondary characteristic:** Freedom of historical difference from he medium of diffusion.
- **Culture core:** Empirical relation between technology and economic factor.
- **Techno-economic factor:** Existence, technology and economy.
- **Natural Environment:** Flora, fauna, minerals, rivers, mountains etc.

NEW CULTURAL ECOLOGY

In the last year of 1960 decade, new theory came in to existence in cultural ecology which is known as new cultural ecology. This new theory is also known as ecological functionalism. The pioneers of this theory are Vayda and Rappaport. Under this new ecological theory culture is not taken as unit of study. Here the unit of study is taken as population. In this theory attention is not paid on lieneal cause and effect relationships, but attention is paid on cybernetics. Here rituals and population control play significant role. Here special attention is paid as to how different elements maintain a balance in population according to their resources. This, adaptational control of resources plays significant role in new cultural ecology.

Rappaport in his book *Pigs for the Ancestors: Rituals in the Ecology of New Guinea People* (1968) has attempted to establish relation between ecology and structural functionalism. He has cited the example of Tschemba tribe of New Guinea. The Tsemba are pig rearers. Pigs are their main resource. They feed pigs the same things which they eat themselves. For domescating pigs they grow more and more foodgrains so that they can feed them. In their cultural system pigs occupied valuable place. They pay pigs as bride price. They fight war. At the end of war, they sacrifice their pigs in the name of ancestors. In this way they control the population of pigs. Thus, domestication and sacrifice of pigs reveal adaptation between culture and environment. The maintenance of the population of pig is essential for them. They maintain it by a cycle. The cycle takes 10 years in completion. In this cycle, war, pig sacrifice and pig reproduction are involved. Here religious rituals and pig sacrifice are cybernetic or non-productive factors. But a balance in ecological system is maintained by it. Rappoport regards culture as function of eco-system.

Vayda was teacher of Rappoport. He had also conducted researches in New Guinea. He was also of view that population should be the ideal unit of analysis, not its culture.

Netting in his book, '*Cultural Ecology*' (1977) has attempted to show the study of cultural ecology on the basis of three approaches which are as follow:

- Eco-system approach
- Ethno-ecology approach
- Historical ecology approach
- Eco-system approach is a central point within cultural ecology.
- Ethno-ecology approach attempts to know cultural ecology from the point of view of ethnic community. For example classificating flora, fauna, river, mountain, soil, season.
- Historical ecology approach examines as to how culture and environment has mutually influenced each other overtime.

MORTON H. FRIED

Morton H. Fried in his famous book, '*Evolution of Political Society*' (1967) has attempted to reproduce the history of origin of civilisation. According to him in the beginning there was egalitarian society. It was a rankless society and there was no stratification. Gradually, rank based society appeared. The rank based society gave rise to social stratification. The complex form of stratification appeared in the state. Sometimes rank and stratification appear together. There are a number of egalitarian societies and rank society. But societies with only stratification are rare. They either move in state society or come back in ranked society. Here emphasis is more on social structure rather than subsistence arrangement. Period could not explain as to how society moved from one stage to another. However, he had made a number of suggestions in this regard such as environmental change and shift in marriage rules.

CULTURAL MATERIALISM

The term materialism appeared in connection to Marxism. Karl Marx and Friedrich Engels had propounded the theory of dialectical materialism which is commonly known as Marxism. The theory of dialectical materialism was different from the theory of cultural materialism. According to the theory of dialectical materialism human existence determines human consciousness contrasted with the idealist belief that human consciousness determines the human existence. In fact they believed that human thoughts, action and institutions are determined by their relationship to the means of production, meaning how a people makes living in material world.

Cultural materialism is a theoretical orientation that distinguishes emic from etic perspectives and mental from behavioural domain, advocating infrastructural determinism.

The theory of cultural materialism was propounded by an American anthropologist Marvin Harris (b.1927). His theory of cultural materialism appears partly in his book, '*The Nature of Cultural Things*' (1964) and '*The Rise of Anthropological Theory*' (1968) and specially in the book, '*Cultural Materialism*' (1979). Like White, Steward and other, Harris also wanted to free anthropological theory from the legacy of Franz-Boas, the founder of American anthropology. He wanted to free anthropology also from the spread of new non-scientific and antiscientific attitudes in profession.

The theory of cultural materialism addresses a central problem for scientific anthropology. According to it people can be both subjects and objects of scientific investigation. People can think and say things about themselves. It is just like as scientists think and say things about them. Now question arises, where does the true knowledge reside? According to Harris, answer can be found by maintaining two parts of cross-cutting epistemological criteria—

- Mental *Versus* behavioural domains
- Emic *Versus* Etic domains.

The mental domain is what people think and the behavioural domain is what people do.

According to Cognitive anthropology, the emic domain belongs to participant and the etic domain belongs to observation.

On combining these two parts of distinction, we get four epistemological perspectives:

- Emic behavioural perspective
- Emic mental perspective
- Etic behavioural perspective
- Etic mental perspective

The emic behavioural perspective is what people think about their own behaviour.

The emic mental perspective is what people think about their own thoughts.

The etic behavioural prespective is what the observer, observes about the behaviours of other people.

The etic mental perspective is what the observer observes about the thoughts of other people.

All four perspectives are possible. But two perspectives are problemetic and can be approached with great caution. The emic behavioural perspective is problematic because people can develop false consciousness and mis-represent the meaning of their own behaviours to themselves and to the others. The etic mental perspective is problematic because it is difficult to find out what is going on inside someone else head. According to Harris emic mental perspective and etic behavioural perspective are more likely to yield meaningful information.

In the scientific anthropology of Harris, both emic and etic perspectives have found place. But he has advised to keep them separate and maintain their own operational definition and data languages. But at the end etic perspective dominates. In the emics perspective the informant is the ultimate judge of the validity. In the etic, the ultimate judge is the scientific observer. Thus, both native and scientists can be objective. But when natives are objectives, they themselves become the scientists. According to Harris, objectivity is not mere intersubjectivity. It is not mitual understanding. It is not an ability to participate in one another's culture. There is only one objective truth—the etic truth of science.

The core of cultural materialism is the principle of infrastructural determinism. According to this principle of Harris, more often than not, culture changes first in etic infrastructure and then reverberates through etic structure and superstructure to affect emic superstructure. Thus, cultural idealists explain culture change as occuring in opposite direction, while cultural eclectics explain culture change consistently.

The cultural materialism of Harris has three parts which are as follows:

- *Infrastructure*: It includes two significant aspects.
- *Mode of Production*: It includes technology and practices employed for expanding or limiting basic subsistence production and other forms of energy.
- *Mode of Reproduction*: This includes technology and practices employed in expanding, limiting and maintaining the population.
- *Structure*: If has two significant aspects.
- *Domestic Economy*: It consists of small number of people who interact on an intimate basis and perform functions like regulating production, basic production, socialisation, education and enforcing domestic discipline.
- *Political Economy*: The groups of political economy may be small or large, but their members do not have emotional commitment to each other. They also perform many functions like regulating reproduction, basic production, socialisation, education and enforcing social discipline.
- *Super Structure*: This consists of following aspects.
- *Behavioural Superstructure*: It includes art, music, dance, literature, rituals, sports, games, hobbies, science.
- *Mental Superstructure*: Traditions, values, emotions beliefs, attitudes.

In his famous article, "The Cultural Ecology of India's Sacred Cattle" (1966), Harris has attempted to deal with the cultural materialism of sacred cattle cow in Indian context. He has described the taboo of beef eating and worship of cow in India as an adaptational behaviour of nature and culture. In India cows are important in so many ways. They give calf, labour, dung and leather. Ecologically, cows are very useful. Therefore, for their preservation taboo on beef eating has been imposed and worship of cows began. Thus, this practice of taboo and worship is adaptation of cows with the culture in materialistic sense. He criticised the classification as useless cattle. No cattle can be useless in an environment. They are useful and economically rational.

Although Harris was greatly influenced by Marx and Engels from whom he had taken the term materialism, but Marx and Engels had omitted mode of reproduction from their formulation. They had confused mental and behavioural and emic and etic realms. They were saddled with Hegelian dialectic—Thesis—antithesis and synthesis. They had not concentrated on scientific principle. When Harris came to know such mistakes in dialectic materialism, he chose to conceptualise his theory of cultural materialism.

In reply of a question why infrastructural determinism?, Harris opines that infrastructure is the primary interface between culture and nature and the place where people start using culture cope with nature in orderly ways.

Like neo evolutionism and new archaeology, the cultural materialism was also pro-science.

HUMAN MATERIALISM

The theory of human materialism was propounded by Paul Magnarella of University of Florida in his book, '*Human Materialism*' (1993). He called his paradigm in human materialism as a model of socio-cultural systems and a strategy for its analysis. He was influenced by the cultural materialism of Marvin Harris. He has also talked about Infrastructure, structure and superstructure. These are different set of contents and relationships in human materialism. Mangnarella has added human dimension to cultural materialism. He included the persons occupying economic and political power within infrastructure. The contributions of charismatic leaders can not be ignored. He argued in favour of readmission of individual level teleology.

Human materialism places human behaviour within its environmental context. It also focusses on human thoughts, plans, strateges and agenda of social leaders.

The Magnarella model of human materialism are as follows:

Infrastructure

- ***Material***—Technology, tools, mode of production, environmental resources and factors.
- ***Human***—Demography, migration, psychological and biological characteristics of people.
- ***Social***—Ownership and control of resources of production.
- ***Social structure***:
  - Family and kinship organisation
  - Social organisation
  - Political, religious and economic organisation
  - Work relation persons with economic and political power.
- ***Super structure***:
  - Ideologies, rituals and symbols associated with various organisation in social structure.
  - Ideologies, rituals and symbols supported by rivals, minorities and marginal members of the population group.

NEW PSYCHOLOGICAL ANTHROPOLOGY

The theory of new psychological anthropology was propounded by John Whiting and Irvin Child in their book, *Child Training and Personality: A Cross-Cultural Study* (1953). But before dealing with their new Psychological anthropological theory, it will be fitness of the context to present here the background of Psychological anthropology.

In many ways Freudian theory represented the very kind of anthropology. Boas and his students were trying to overcome the Freudian theory. Frend's ideas were highly speculative, overly generalised, evolutionary, hereditarian, sexist and in equating non-Western adults with Western children racist and ethnocentric. Boas had used Margaret Mead to disapprove the Universality of Adolescent Psycho-sexual turmoil. Britsh Social Anthropologist Brownis Law Slavo Kaspar Malinowski had also rejected the Freudian concept of

Oedepus complex. It was irrelevent for matrilineal south Pacific Trobriand islanders. In the society of Trobriand islanders mother's brother was soul authority not the father over sons. Empirical evidences were not supporting the Freudian theory. If it was to be accepted the whole theoretical framework was to be reconstructed with cross-cultural variables.

While finding Freudian theory objectionable, the Boasian anthropologists had found it stimulating and engaging. Like anthropology, Freudian Psychology was iconoclastic forcing people to analyse facts and behaviour which they usually accepted as normal. It was a body of thought about personality, a subject in which anthropology could claim no special expertise. Psychological anthropolgists were attracted towards Freudian Psychology in 1930s, but they had changed it in major ways. They had abandoned Freud's explanation of Psychic evolution. They had down played his emphasis on sex and had recasted his own formulation interms of cultural relativism. They had focused on the development of normal personality as opposed abnormal or pathological personality. The result was a new Freudian phase in Psychological anthropology. This phase marked the study of development of personality cross-culturally with a strong emphasis on the importance of early childhood experiences.

The chief theoretical architect of Freudian Anthropology was Abam Kardiner, a Psychoanalist who studied with Freud, but realised that Freud's ideas were culture bound. To accomplish this task in the late 1930s, he conveyed a seminar at Newyork of Anthropologists. Boasian Ruth Benedict, Ruth Bunzel, Edward Sapir and CoraDu-Bois were participants of the Seminar. The objective of the seminar was to develop a theoretical framework for investigating how different cultural experiences nurtured different personality types. With input from Seminar, Kardiner devised a research model with three major components: Primary cultural institution, secondary cultural institutions and basic personality structure. Primary institutions were institutions that affected child rearing practices. For example feeding, weaning and daily care of infacts. Secondary institutions were major institutions of society such as, politics, and religion. In Kardiner's model, basic personality structure was shaped by primary institutions and then projected on to secondary institutions which functioned to help people cope with the world by depicting the world in familiar culturally adaptive terms. Kardiner has called this approach Psychodynamic. The task of Psychodynamic research was to assess primary institutions, secondary institutions, and basic personality structure independently and then to correlate them in terms of Kardiner's model.

To assess basic personality structure, psychodynamic anthropologists used clinical tests like Thematic Apperception Test (TAT) and Rorschach or ink blot test to get informants project their personalities on paper. The first systematic research of this kind was done by Cora Du Bois (1903-1991) on the island of Alor in the Dutch East Indies. Du Bois collected Rorschach profiles, children's drawing and Psychological life histories. They were sent back to clinical specialists in New York for assessment. These specialists concluded that the basic Alorese personality was shallow, indifferent and apathetic. According to Du Bois it was developed from the early childhood personality experience of maternal neglect caused by Alorese mothers need to spend extended periods of time away from their children tending crops in the field. This neglect taught children that their emotional needs would not be readily satisfied. Low expectation were projected in to Alorese religion, characterised by unresponsive duties and carelessly manufactured effigies. Shaped through this kind of projection, alorese religion was able to help children adapt to maternal neglect children received. Du Bois called such basic personality as model personality because they were derived from tests and clinical assessments. Her book, *People of Alore* (1942) was the theoretical high points of Psychodynamic anthropology.

The theoretical low points of psychodynamic anthropology were the national character studies in Second World War era. These studies had marked the end of serious blend of anthropology and Freudian theory. Innovations in social scientific research methods particularly the increased use of statistics beginning in the 1950s, prompted anthropologists to distance themselves from Freudian Psychology. Freudian Psychology from the perspective of empirical science appeared as ill defined and uninvestigatable concept.

A new generation of Psychological anthropologists began to use statistics to make cross-cultural generalisations precise. The pioneering effort in this new direction was made by John Whiting and Irvin Child in their book, *Child Training and Personality: Across-cultural Study* (1953). Whiting and Childe generated cross-cultural data from other sources, the New Human Relations Area File at Yale University and manipulated these data statistically to reveal significant cross-cultural associations. One statistically significant cross-cultural association, described by Marvin Harris in his book, *Rise of Anthropological Theory* involved the following tracts:

Prolonged period of nursing of mother's breast, prolonged post-partum prohibitions of sexual intercourse, polygeny, or practice of a man having more than one wife, infants sleeping with mothers, patrilineality and patrilocality, determination of genealogical descent, post-marital residence from male line and strong male puberty rites.

In statistics, association does not necessarily imply cause, but statistical association can suggest cause and help narrow the search for cause effect relationships. Anthropologists have been abie to link Whiting and Child traits in cause and effect chain of events beginning with the need for prolonged period of nursing to supplement dietary protein, and ending with the need for strong male puberty rites to seize the close attachment of son to mother in cultures with male domination.

Whiting and child modified Kardiner's Psychodynamics model and renounced its major components. They modified the Kardiner's Primary institutions as maintenance system because they affected child training practices. They modified secondary institutions as projective systems and basic personality structure as personality variables.

Right from coming of Age in Samoa to child training and personality: A cross-cultural study, in 25 years the American Psychological anthropology evolved through Pre-Freudian, Freudian and post-Freudian phases. A brand of anthropology that began as humanistic almost literary attempt to make Americans more tolerant of culture and personality differences ended up in the middle of twentieth century following the lead of psychologically detached social science.

2
Structural Anthropology (Structuralism)

Introduction

The pioneer of structural anthropology or theory of structuralism was Claude Levi-Strauss, a French social-cultural anthropologist. His theory of structuralism is quite different from the structural functionalism of A.R. Radcliffe-Brown and his followers. The theory of structural-functionalism was based on organic model, whereas theory of structuralism was based on linguistic model. The intellectual transition from Durkheim to Claude Levi-Strauss and French structural anthropology was accomplished by Durkheim's student and nephew Marcel Mauss. Therefore, it is worth mentioning here the contributions of Emile Durkheim and Marcel Mauss before dealing with the contribution of Levi-Strauss.

EMILE DURKHEIM (1858-1917)

When Franz Boas and his followers were promulgating their brands of anthropology in North America, other anthropological theoretical influences were at work in France and Britain. Classical cultural evolutionism had never took hold in France. That is why when French anthropology assumed its twentieth century identity, it had nothing to reject its nineteenth century legacy. Rather theoretical foundation of twentieth century French anthropology can be found in nineteeth century French Socialogist Emile Durkheim. Durkheim had a major influence on key British anthropologists of early twentieth century particularly Alfred Reginald Radcliffe Brown and his theory of structural-functionalism. It is because of this reason, Durkheimis considered as forerunner of two European schools known as French structural anthropology and British social anthropology.

Durkheim's theories develoed in progression with the publication of four books: *Division of Labour in Society* (1893), *The Rules of Sociological Method* (1895), *Suicide* (1897), and *The Elementary Forms of the Religious Life* (1912). Each book added in ingredient to the recipes for French and British school.

If his book, '*Division of Labour*', Durkheim has explored the diversification and integration of culture, indentifying two integrative patterns: older more primitive cultures were less deversifised and had little division of labour, more homogeneous, they cohered because individuals were similar. Durkheim has called this pattern of integration as mechanical solidarity. Recent, more civilised cultures were more diversified, had considerable division of labour, more heterogenous, they cohered because individuals were different. His vision was of individuals functioning independently, but in harmony. Durkheim has called this pattern of integration as organic solidarity. Durkheim was of opinion that Social Solidarity could be achieved in two different organisationally opposite ways. His focus was on coherence rather than change, represented as a preference what August Comte called social statics rather than social dynamics. Durkheimian verson of society was different from the version of Karl Marx who saw solidarity as ephemeral and society riven with class conflict. Accordingly to Marx, state would gradually witheraway and give rise to communism. For Durkheim more organic solidarity increased, the more Government was necessary to regulate life. Socially, inter-dependent parts, increased organic solidarity, submerged the individual in an expanded social reality. It is because social interactions superseded individual interactions as determinants of social life. The academic discipline which would studies the social interactions was sociology.

Durkheim established the theoretical framework for sociology in his book, '*Rules of Sociological Method*'. He was of opinion that social interaction could be considered as social facts and explained interms of other social facts; not interms of biology or Psychology. Behind this prouncement was Durkheim's understanding that society was a realm unto itself, sui generis. It was something like A.L.

Kroeber's concept of superorganic. But Durkheim gave his conception of social facts a special French twist. For him social facts were collective representation of collective consciousness or group mind. This conception was Cartesian, following the rationalist Freach Philosopher Rene Descartes, rather than Lockan following the empiricist British Philosopher John Locke. Rationalism became the fundamental part of Durkheimian legacy to French structural anthropology.

In his book, '*Suicide*' Durkheim demonstrated as to how sociological rule can be used to explain particular social facts. He chose the fact of suicide because it was an act that seemed so individualistic, yet it could be explained sociologically because it has a strong social diversion. Durkheim correlated types of suicide with social integration. With mechnical solidarity, there was altruistic suicide, whereby individuals dissolved themselves into homogeneous group with organic solidarily, there was egostic suicide, whereby individuals engaged in a dramatic form of self-expression. When society was in flux, neither mechanical nor organic, individuals could commit a third type of suicide, anomie, Durkheim's name for the sense of alienation, caused by absence of familiar social norms.

In his book, '*Elementary form of Religious Life*' Durkkheim attempted to expose the origins of religion. To Durkheim, origin meant something very different than it meant to cultural evolutionists, historical particularist and other kinds of anthropologists whose orientation was diachronic and who considered the origin of something to be its source in past. For Durkheim the source of origin was not past, but in the group mind. Accordingly, the elementary forms of religious life were collective representation of the collective consciousness of the people; who attached sacred meaning to moral principle and gave those moral principles a social reality in order to make them persuasive. Empiricists have found Durkheim's logic circular: collective representation demonstrate the existence of collective consciousness; which is posited to demonstrate the existence of collective representations. But Durkheim was not an empiricist. He was rationalist. He believed that knowledge could be independent of observation. Rationalism was imparted to French structural anthropology when elementary forms of religion of Durkheim became the elementary structure of kinship of Levi-Strauss.

For Durkheim the origin of religion, and ultimately society itself, lay in the impact of ritual on individuals. His thesis was that primitive man experiences a sense of effervescence when interacting with his fellow that can only be accounted for by reference to greater power existing out side of individual. Once the ritual has ended and large clan would have broken into small bands and dispersed to resume the mundane activities associated with making a living. Durkheim enshired this distinction between the every day and the ritual in his oppositional concepts sacred and profane. These terms are appropriate, because they convey the forms of activity and emotions that surround the pure and powerful occasions of ritual togetherness. It is opposed to those that indicate routine, the mundane, he, and the polluted. Durkheim showed as to how effervescent sensations born in rituals were embodied in totem. Totems are powerful representation of elementary forms, which bring these powerful sentiment to the surface of consciousness, even in the absence of ritual. Thus, according to Durkheim the religion originated as a social fact and created dualities such as sacred and profane. Beliefs and rituals were added to sacred sentiment. It was accepted by group mind through rituals. In the elementary forms of religious life, the concept of God and society seem interchangeable.

MARCEL MAUSS (1872-1950)

The intellectual transition from Durkheim to Claude Levi-Strauss and French structural anthropology was accomplished by Marcel Mauss. He was a student and nephew of Emile Durkheim. Like his uncle he sought to reduce social facts to elementary structures. In his essay, *The Gift* (1924), he shifted Durkheim's focus from mind of Group to mind of individuals. In his scheme, elementary structures of individual minds precede elementary structure of group mind, which inturn precede elementary structure of the outside world. Mauss was interested in elementary structure of practice of giving gifts. For him, the practice of gift giving is exchange or reciprocity which operates according to elementary principles "to give, to receive and to repay". Reciprocity is ingrained mental structure, a logic shared by every one. Unlike economic anthropologists, who consider reciprocity to be restricted to non-market economic transactions, Mauss considered it to be universal principle of exchange governing social organisation and kinship, besides economic transactions. This was the idea eleborated upon by Levi-Strauss.

CLAUDE LEVI-STRAUSS (1908-2009)

Claude Levi-Strauss is regarded as *Guru* (founder teacher) of French structural anthropology. He is one of the most celebrated, even not always understood, anthropologists of the twentieth century. During his years as students, he was interested in politics, but pushed the tradition established by French ethnography and Marcel Mauss forward. After field work in Brazel, he turned his attention towards the anthropological theory. Dealing with anthropological theory, he published his two important book, *Elementary Structure of Kinship* (1949) and *Structural Anthropology* (1963). These two books present a complex analysis of kinship based on receprocity, the reciprocal exchange of women.

Following the tradition of solidarity established by Emile Durkheim, Levi-Strauss began with the preposition that reciprocal exchange of women in kinship system promoted alliance. The promotion of alliance facilitated social interaction and made society cohere. These alliances were achieved through reciprocal exchange of women as 'gift'. According to Levi-Strauss the structure for gift giving is innate in the human mind. It operates with a universal logic of dualities called binary oppositions. Levi-Strauss had learnt about binary oppositions from the Prague school of structural linguists, led by linguist Roman Jacobson. He had formulated the concept of phonemes. In structural linguistic phonemes are minimally contrasting pairs of sounds that create linguistic meaning. In structural anthropology, binary oppositions are contrasting pairs of mental constructs that create social meaning. Some of examples of binary oppositions are life *versus* death, nature *versus* culture and self *versus* others. With binary oppositions, the relationship between elements is as important as the elements themselves. This relationship is mediated. For example the binary opposition between kingroups, a transformation of binary opposition of self *versus* other, is mediated by exchange of women. In structural anthropology or structuralism, binary oppositions are parts of an integrated system of logically connected categories of meaning that structure social activity and the way activities are conceptualised.

Levi-Strauss has analysed social organisation in the same way as structural linguists have analysed the language. Here form is as important as content. In elementary structure of kinship, kinship groups who exchange a woman create a form of relationship among themselves as well as relationship among exchanged women. This relationship helps to mediate the group. It brings them closer together.

Implicated in exchanges of women are four basic relationships.

- Brother and sister
- Husband and wife
- Father and son
- Mother's brother or uncle and sister's son or nephew.

Each of these relationship is either positive or promoting harmony and happiness or negative promoting hostility and antagonism. But it is mind which balance positives and negatives. Thus, in a given exchange system two relationships must be positive and two must be negative. The content of relationships can change from culture to culture, but their form or logic or structure remains the same.

According to Levi-Strauss, the exchange of women assumes either of two forms:

- Restricted exchange
- Generalised exchange

Restricted exchange creates a relationship of two kinship groups through symmetrical cross-cousin marriages. In symmetrical cross-cousin marriage, whereby brothers and sisters in one group marry cross cousins, cousins related through parents of opposite sex in other group. Generalised exchange creates a relationship between more than two kin groups through asymmetrical cross cousin marriage. In asymmetrical cross-cousin marriage, brothers and sisters are not exchanged between two groups, directly, but return to their groups after having been circulated through other groups. But the generalised exchange promotes more solidarity than restricted exchange. It is because it creates alliances involving more kingroups.

Levi-Strauss has identified two forms of generalised exchanges: Matrilateral and patrilateral. Matrilateral exchange promotes more social solidarity than patrilateral exchange. Matrilateral cross-cousin marriage is more prevalent-than the patrilateral cross-cousin marriage in the ethnographic record.

Besides kinship, Levi-Strauss has made a substantial theoretical contribution on myths, savage mind and food preferences.

In analysing the North American myth of the "tricky coyote", Levi-Struass has set-up two pairs of analogous binary oppositions agriculture is to warfare as life is to death. Here hunting mediates agriculture and warfare because hunting preserves life of man while leads to death to animals. Scavenging animals like, the Koyote mediate an another pair of binary oppositions, *herbivore carnivore* also analogous to life and death. Therefore, Koyote must be tricky.

In his book, '*The Raw and Cooked*', (1969), Levi-Strauss has contrasted the raw, cooked and rotted food. The book is devoted to the structure of cuisine for cooked food, boiling is to roasting as culture is to nature. Boilded foods are served to kins and roasted foods are served to strangers. Kins are associated with culture, while strangers are associated with nature.

Edmund Leach has provided an another example of structural analysis. According to him religion is an attempt to bridge the structural opposition between life and death by creation of concept of another world.

Levi-Strauss has dealt with myths on the same dualities of nature and culture.

STRUCTURAL MARXISM

The Franch structural anthropology had also influenced the followers of Marxism. Under the influence of structural anthropology the concept of structural Marxism came into existence. Under the influence of Levi-Strauss, structural Marxism developed during the 1970s as an effort to dematerialise Marxism. The structural Marxists dematerialised the theory of dialectical materialism and focussed on the structure of dialectical thought. Thought as opposed to behaviour is implicated by the Marxist concepts of class consciousness and social relations of the means of economic production. The above implications were elaborated by a group of structural Marxists led by Maurice Godelier.

Structural Marcism also came into existence as an anthropological debate that began during 1960s, between economic formalists and economic sustantivists. Formalists like Scott Cook maintained that the traditional Western definition of economics, the allocation of scare resources among unlimited want, is also applied to non-Western economics. Substantivists like George Dalton, Karl Polanyi and Marshal Sahlins expressed their disagreements. They critcised formalists as ethnocentric. They were of view that capitalist conception, could not be applied to economics lacking markets and political apparatus of state. According to substantivists, people in cultures governed by kinship do not think like economic materialists and strategize to maximise their material advantages. It is because the primary significance of their economic transactions is social. Some Substantivists even argued that economic exploitation does not exists unless people think that they are being exploited. Persuing such ideas, structural Marxists like Jonathan Freudman began searching for hidden structures called as dialectical structures that make economics trick. Freudman found that the structure of capitalist economies is fetish for money, while the structures of non-capitalist economies are rooted in social and religious values. Sahlins in his book, '*Islands of History*' (1987) promoted his notion of structure as historically objectified relation of cultural order. The main thrust of structural Marxism has been to transform the theory of dialectical materialism into a theory of dialectical idealism by demonstrating that the structure of economic transactions derives from the structure of thought.

3
Biologised Anthropology

Introduction

In order to understand anthropology as a whole or in totality, it is essential to know about social-cultural anthropology, Biological anthropology, prehistoric archeological anthropology and Linguistic anthropology. Although in America these four main branches of anthropology were taught under the subject anthropology since beginning. The founder of American anthropology Franz Boas had started such four field wholistic approach in anthropology. But social cultural anthropology had influence on other branches of anthropology. A good number of anthropologists belonged to social-cultural anthropology. Attention was not paid on relation between social-cultural anthropology and biological anthropology. Biological anthropology was almost neglected. But after 1960 the situation changed and the relation between social cultural anthropology and biological anthropology took a positive turn.

The main cause of this positive change in relation between social-cultural anthropology and biological anthropology was emergence interest in biological base of human behaviour. In the primary observation of social biologists many favourite subjects were regarded as genetic. For example genetic factors related to aggressiveness, regionality and sexuality. The examples of such type of style can be Robert Adrey books, *African Genesis* (1961) and *Territorial Imperative* (1966) and Desmond Morris book, *Naked Ape* (1967). The authors of these books were disapproved by both social-cultural anthropologists and biological anthropolists. They were disapproved because they lacked scientific explanation. Their approach was based on naked apery. Although anthropologists were forced to think that what should be the truth of biological base of human behaviour, while criticising the naked apery. In 1960, two significant confusion arose regarding biological base of race. Biological anthropologist Karleton Coon's book. *The Origins of Race* was published in 1963. In this book Coon had proposed that there were five geographical races of Homosapien species. They were evolved from Homoerectus. Caucasoid (White) race had attained to Homosapien status first of all and the Nigro got Homosapien status in the last. At that time Coon was at regarded as a follower of scientific racism. He was criticised on this ground.

Another anthropological confusion had arisen from the proposal of educational psychologist Arthur Jensen that difference in intelligence quotient had genetic base. 15 point I.Q. difference prevalent in American black and white cannot be removed by education. This proposal was also rejected by anthropologists. Critics of racism termed it as Jensenism. But some anthropologist found the proposal of Jensen true. In fact, they supported the view of Jensen. According to them Jensen was criticised due to ideological difference, not on the basis of scientificity. Biological base of human behaviour was accepted as a theme of scientific investigation. Due to differences in scientific and political views on proposal of Robert Ardrey, Desmmud Moris, Carleton Coon and Arthur Jensen, social-cultural anthropologists and biological anthropologist came closer. As a result—new biological anthropology was established. Neo biological anthropology was neither concerned with cultural anthropology, nor with prehistoric anthropology. S. Wash Burn had encouraged physical anthropologists to adopt synthetic theory of evolution. Within synthetic theory advice was given to adopt synthesis of Darwinism and Mendelism. Biologists had accepted this synthesis in the decade of 1930. But it was accepted in biological anthropology in the decade of 1960. Following synthetic theory attempt was made to study biological process in place of form in biological anthropology. Alongwith this, suggestions were accepted to give up symbolic and classificatory views. This change in the mentality of biological anthropologists was gladly accepted by social-cultural anthropologists. Biological anthropologists had given up the idea of pure race. In the mean time cultural analysis of geographical distribution of Sickle Cell Anemia and Lactose (milk sugar) was made by biological anthropologists. As a result of this explanatory success, Bio-cultural anthropology emerged as a new area of study and research in anthropology. The main aim of bio-cultural anthropology was to search inter-relationship between culture and human biology according to evolutionary theory. Being encouraged with this relationship, some anthropological gladly accepted to explain the biological base of cultural behaviour.

In the 1970 decade, four bio-cultural approaches were developed which laid great impact on anthropology. They are as follows:

- Medical Anthropology
- Behavioural Genetics
- Socio-biology

Medical Anthropology: In this new area of anthropology cross-cultural and Pan-historical study of health and illness is done. This area of anthropology was related externally to geneticity of human behaviour. In its theory there was unity and no conflict.

Behavioural Genetics: This grew out of animal psychology and zoology. It involved a more strict commitment to hereditarian concepts such as fixed action pattern, innate releasing mechanism and key stimulus. Human ethologists examined both ontogeny (individual growth) and phylogeny (evolutionary growth) of biologically linked behaviours that constituted human biogram in the language of human ethology. According to ethologists cultural universals like facial expressions and gestures were potentially genetic.

A diluted form of ethology found its way in to the anthropological study of non-verbal communication or body language in the sciences of kinesics and prosemics. Kinesies is science which deals with the motion of body. It studies human body motion scientifically. Prosemics is a science which deals with the study of human body positioning. Anthropologists like Lionel Tiger and Robin Fox promoted a diluted form of ethology in books like *Men in Group* (1970) and *The Imperial Animal* (1971). In these books they expounded their views on natural human tendencies. Many critics ended up using the adjective ethological to describe any proposition that attributed human behaviour to heredity.

The third bio-behavioural approach to come of age in 1970s was the behaviour genetics. It was an extension of genetic analysis from anatomy and physiology to behaviours. The behavioural genetics treat it as phenotype or product of geneaction. The behavioural geneticists study both normal and abnormal behaviour phenotypes in order to determine whether they might have eeither a simple Mendelian or a more complex polygenic component. Human behavioural geneticists rely on contrasts of behaviours of twins reared together and apart to help them assign the sources of behavioural differences to nature and nurture. Arthur Jensen's investigation of race, genes and I.Q. employed some of these techniques. But behavioural genetics never reached its full potential to prove controversy in anthropology.

Socio-biology: The bio-behavioural approach that made the greatest in roads in late twentieth century anthropology was socio-biology. Socio-biology is an investigation of biological basis of social behaviour using the evolutionary principles of kin selection and inclusive fitness. It is an examination to find out biological basis of social behaviour. The anthropologists interested in biological basis of social behaviour formed a school known as socio-biology. Socio-biology makes study of use of evolutionary biology on social behaviour, Socio-biology makes systematic study of all kinds of social behaviour in all organisms. It tries to find out and explain basic pattern with the help of evolution.

Socio-biologists have attempted to find out solutions of some questions. These questions are what is evolutionary history of a behaviour? What is adaptational value of behaviour ? Whether the behaviour of organism are such that they could maintain their fitness more and more?

According to Darwin, every individual has more relation with his survivals. But Socio-biologists are of opinion that survival is not only related to an individual. It is related to the whole population. Success of survivals can be measured on the basis of fitness. Thus, fitness is a measure of evolutionary success. Fitness is related to reproduction and fertile efficiency. The individuals who reproduce more and more offspring, are termed as fittest from the point of view of evolution. Because their offsprings produce more and more off springs on being young and adult. According to Darwin the behaviour of each individual (he/she) is to maintain his/her maximum fitness. Socio-biologists have carried forward this view.

Socio-biologists have accepted this fact that all animals behave to maximise their fitness. According to recent theories fitness has, many layers. When fitness is related to individual (he/she), it is known as individual fitness. When fitness is related to parents and offsprings, it is known as inclusive fitness. When fitness is related to kins, it is known as kin selection and when fitness is related to a group, it is known as group selection. Socio-biologists deal with following types of behaviour:

- Altruism
- Eusociality
- Cooperation
- Reciprocation
- Selfish
- Spite

Altruism: It is a social behaviour which curtails the individual fitness propounded by Darwin and increase the recipient fitness. According to Darwin individual behaves for his/her fitness. But behaviour of altruism or selflessness reveals that individual performs such behaviour for the benefit of his/her relatives. Levontin (1970) conducted an observation on rabbits and showed that a rabbit sacrifice its food and residence for the benefit of its relative rabbit. In order to facilitate reproduction of other relative by sacrificing own reproduction is known as altruism or selflessness.

Eusociolity: When an individual sacrifices his/her own reproductive facility in order to raise his/her own other relatives' reproduction is known as eusociality. For example beehieve where other female bees sacrifice their reproductive fitness to increase the reproductive fitness of queen bee. They remain barren, but increase the reproduction of queen bee.

Cooperation: Related animals extend help to each other at the time of trouble. Among birds and monkeys cooperative child rearing is found. Wolves, wild dogs, crocodiles and seal fishes, wallras and parasite animals do cooperative hunting. The flock of same birds make an attack on snake. The group of same monkeys face collectively the parasites. Cooperation is a collective process in which every individuals are benefited.

Reciprocation: There is exchange of services among animals. Healthy dolphin extends help to ill dolphin to bring the ill dolphin on the surface of water so that it could breath air. When the healthy dolphin falls ill, the other dolphin which was benefited by its service extends full help to it. In this way reciprocal exchange of services takes place among animals.

Selfish: Animals are selfish, too. They take revenge, too. In selfish behaviour the primary one is beneficial and the recipient is looser. The young male gibbon who defeats the old male leader of the group and becomes the leader of the entire group, kills all kids surviving on breast feeding. This behaviour is done to make females excrete dimbs so that, he could produce his own offsprings. This is a selfish behaviour.

Spite: Some animals destroy its own fitness to destory the fitness of the others. For example struggle between two he buffaloes or two bulls.

SOCIO-BIOLOGICAL EXAMINATION

As referred to earlier, socio-biology is an examination in which biological base of social behaviour is found out. In order to find out biological face of social behaviour evolutionary theories like kin selection and inclusive fitness have been followed. Although socio-biology came into existence in twentieth century, but this approach had become controversial ever since publication of Edward O, Wilson landmark book, *Socio-biology: The New Synthesis* (1975). Wilson was a Harward University entomologist who had worked on evolutionary problem of altruism or self-sacrificing behaviours, such as sterile workers devoting themselves to helping a queen to reproduce. The problem of altruism was how to explain it interms of Darwinian evolution by natural selection. If altruistic behaviour is genetic, it shall be subject to the action of natural selection. But the result of such action should be the reduction or elimination of genes responsible. Still altruism persisted. How? Earlier biologists had proposed the mechanism of group selection whereby individuals sacrifice for the good of the group, as group numbers benefit indirectly. This mechanism was never convincing entirely. In early 1970, a number of geneticists proposed the alternative mechanism of kin selection. This mechanism had become the scientific corner stone of Wilson's book.

Wilson had solved the problem of altruism essentially by defining it out of existence. Altruism is not really altruistic, it is selfish. He defined altruism as selfish with his new concept of inclucive fitness. According to him, the genetic basis of most behaviours is polygenic. Polygenic means variation in pheno type affected by the action of multiple genes. Genetic relatives share these genes. Therefore, individuals who sacrifice themselves can still transmit their sacrificing genes to future generations, as long as they sacrifice themselves for relatives.

Socio-biology is also known as biology of Nepotism. Because Socio-biologists predict that genes incline individuals to behave more favourally to relatives than to non-relatives and more favourably to close relatives than to distant relatives. In this way individuals maximize their inclusive Darwinian fitness and reproductive success. Evolutionary biologist Richard Dawkins had dealt with many of these ideas in his controversial book *The Selfish Gene* (1976).

In the view of socio-biology, life is a series of strategic choices in which individuals unconsciously assess the personal cost and benefit of alternative behaviour and end up choosing the alternative with greatest inclusive yield. Because over all degrees of genetic relatedness can be quantified. Parents and children share 50 per cent of their genes, half siblings 25 per cent genes, first consin 12.5 per cent and so on. Socio-biologists can make precise predictions about behaviour and compare them with empirical reality. Socio-biologists Robert-Trivers introduced the supplementary evolutionary mechanism of reciprocal altruism to explain altruism in non-relatives.

The most controversial pronouncements of socio-biology was differences between males and females. Both males and females are motivated to maximize their inclusive fitness, but in fundamentally different ways. In bisexual reproducing species like mammals, males produce a large number of mobile speremes, but do not themselves bear children. On the other hand females produce a small number of non-mobile eggs, but themselves bear children. These biological differences imply the evolution of behavioural differences. Males are selected to compete for females because females are reproductively relevent resource. The reproductive potential of males depends on number of females they can inseminate. On the other hand, females are selected to resist male advance, because, once inseminated, they cannot become pregnant again until after giving birth. The reproductive potential of females depends on quality not the quantity of male suitors. By depicting males as sexually indiscriminate and females as choosey, Socio-biologists exposed themselves to the criticism that they were affirming Western sex role stereotype. By proposing that both males and females preferred their own kind over foreigners, Socio-biologists exposed themselves to the further criticism that they were racists and xenophotic, fear and dislike of foreigners.

Wilson's book contained only one chapter devoted to some extent on human socio-biology, while remaining chapters were devoted to insects and other non-human animals species. The final chapter deals with as to how socio-biology might account for some of behaviours of Homosapiens. Later on, Wilson along with other socio-biologists refined their speculations. They developed a sealed down modified verson of human socio-biology. Human socio-biology had provoked a strong opposition in anthropology. It was because culture was held more important than biology as the determinants of behavioural differences. Cultural anthropologists, cultural materialists and structralists unitedly criticised human socio-biology. They criticised it as irrelevent and condemn it as disguised ideology of social Darwinism. This was the opinion of majority of cultural anthropologists towards human socio-biology.

A small number of cultural anthropologists like Yanomamo Indian ethnographer Nepolean Chagnon had adopted the human socio-biological perspectives. In primatology socio-biology has become a dominant research strategy.

4
Cognitive Anthropology

Introduction

The School of Anthropology concerned with folk taxonomies and Semantic domains is known as cognitive anthropology. It is deeply related to ethno-linguistics and ethno-science. Ethno linguistics is an approach derived from the linguistically oriented methods of cognitive anthropology. Ethno-science is a term for the collection of methods used in cognitive anthropology. Cognitive anthropology is also related to New ethnography. When the methodologies of ethno-science and ethno-linguistics were infact new, the term New ethnography was used to describe cognitive anthropology. One can understand the whole theoretical background of cognitive anthropology in terms of following concepts:

- Preference of Emic Over Etic
- Sapir-Whorf Hypothesis
- Folk Taxonomies and Semantic Domain
- Componential analysis

Four or five decades after the death of Max Weber, his legacy in anthropology was realised. As mid-1920th Century anthropology in America was expanded and diversified, a number of new theoretical approaches were emerged either as continuation of or reactions to Boasian historical particularism. One such approach was cognitive anthropology.

PREFERENCE OF EMIC OVE ETIC

Infact cognitive anthropology was rooted in Boasian cultural relativism with input from anthropological linguistics. Its theoretical orientation was emic not etic. In anthropology the contrast between emics and etics came into existence in 1950s. It as linguist Kenneth Pike who made an analogy with distiction between emics and etics (1954) in linguistics. According to him phonemics is the study of linguistic meaning, while phonetics is the study of linguistic sounds. Linguistics can study the sound system of languages by themselves with language speakers supplying raw data. To discover which sounds are meaningful, they rely on language speakers as authorities Phonetics represents the point of view of outsiders, the linguist investigator. Phonemics represents the point of view of insider, the speaker being investigated. The contrast between emics and etics can be understood by citing the example of participant observation.

According to Pike, the observation was etic and the participation was emic. The participation was emic, because in principle its goal was to think and behave like natives. Observation was etic because its goal was to have anthropologists remain detached. The emic approach was seeing things from the native's point of view. According to Pike, this appraoch was suitable for promoting cross-cultural understanding and combating ethnocentrism in accordance with the doctrine of cultural relativism. Pike had advocated both emic and etic approaches of anthropology, but he had preferred emic approach over etic approach.

SAPIR-WHORF HYPOTHESIS

The proposition that the structure of language and the structure of thought correspond with the structure of language preponderant is known as Sapir-Whorf hypothesis. Sapir-Whorf hypothesis was another source of cognitive anthropology. It was named after anthropological linguist Edward Sapir and his associate Benjamin Lee Whorf. The Sapir was a student of Boas. He was also a close friend of Ruth Benedict and Margaret Mead. He was fully nurtured and trained under Boasian tradition. He used to create poetry and explore the relation between personality and culture. He was talented both artistically and mathematically. Sapir had devoted most of his career to the study of language. First in Canada, then at the University of Chicago and finally at Yale University, where he had co-founded the Anthropology Department. Whorf used to work for an insurrance company in Harlford, not too far from Yale in new Heaven. Here he met with Edward Sapir. Under the imfluence of Sapir, Whorf developed a hypothesis about the relationship between culture and personality in the 1930s. This hypothesis was formulated under the collaboration of Sapir and Whorf. That is why it is known as Sapir Whorf hypthesis.

According to Sapir-Whorf hypothesis, mental structures of languages and cultures are correlated. The structures of languages influence the structure of cultures and *vice-versa*—Sapir and Whorf were specially interested in the influence of language on culture. They cited an example of contrast between Hopi language and culture and combination of European language and cultures called Standard Average European or SAE. In SAE the concept of time is objectified as by being quantified in expressions such five days, two weeks, six months, one year etc. In contrast Hopi language is subjectified by lacking quantification in expressions. They express time as a process of being later such as when will he come. Is he coming, he or she has become young, they have grown old and so on.

The SAE language also uses objective mass nouns or materials nouns such as milk, water, food and so on. In SAE material nouns are objectified as some water, some food or a glass of milk etc. In contrast Hopi languages lacks material (mass) nouns. Here every noun is individualised, rendering it subjective without the need of quantification for example you eat, she ate, He drank, etc.

SAE speakers objectify the concept of space by using spatial metaphors in rhetorical expressions such as make a point, grasp an idea, come straight to conclusion. In contrast Hopi speakers subjectify space with special parts of speech called tensors. In each of these cases, the contrast between the structure of SAE and Hopi language is correlated with a contrast between objectifying SAE and subjectifying Hopi cultures which structure the world differently. Sapir and Whorf believed that culture is carried around in people's head as a classificatory logic that creates meaning. Different cultures have different meaning systems; which like phonemic systems of language are equally worthy yet mutually in comprehensive in the absence of a means of cross-cultural communication. This is also kown as linguistic relativism.

FOLK TAXONOMIES AND SEMANTIC DOMAINS

When a fraction of American anthropologists sought to make their emic orientation explicit inpired by linguists, cognitive anthropology emerged in 1960s. They improved their methodological regour. This school was known as Ethno-Science, ethno-linguistics and New ethnography. This school is known for its investigative techniques deviced mainly by practiceners Harold Conklin, Charles Frake and Ward Good Enough. The object of this technique was to describe native cognition or perception as a Semantic Domain or domain of meaning with a cognitive "Code" and could be cracked or decoded.

The folk taxonomies of meaning resembles with the Linnaean taxonomy of Western biology. The Linnaean Taxonomy is a classification of realm of living things using hierarchy of categories defined by biological criteria. Likewise, folk taxonomics were classification of cultural realms using hierarchies of categories defined by cultural criteria.

Cognitive anthropology shares views that culture is a formal system of rules for thought and behaviour. Unlike in western biology, where Linnaean classfication is held true and folk classifications of living things wrong. But in cognitive anthropology both classifications were treated as culture dependent.

Harold Koklin (1955) studied the colour categorization among the Hanunoo in Philipines. He found a significant difference in ways in which Hanunoo classified colours as compared to Western categorisation. Hanunoo use moisture, surface texture and lightness as the critical attributes for naming the colour. But Western categorisation of colour is based on hue, brightness and saturation.

Vein, Frake (1961) studied the cultural classification of diseases among the Subanum of Mindanio in Southern Philipines. Subanum has their own cultural criteria for classifying diseases such as age, sex, general, reproduction.

Following the folk taxonomies approach attempts have been made to understand the cultural critaria for classifying things and events such as land, water, house, household articles, plants, animals, food, crops, supernatural entities, arts, crafts, knowledge, institutions, associations, stature, illness, treatment and therapy. On the basis of cultural criteria, cognitive anthropologists have attempted to achieve a meaningful cultural analysis.

COMPONENTIAL ANALYSIS

Componential analysis is a major method of cognitive anthropology used to generate folk Taconomies of a semantic domain. Ward Good Enough (1956) is regarded as pioneer of componential analysis in anthropology. Componential analysis method is also known as feature analysis method. He has taken his clues from the language. He did not examine the inter psychological state. He focussed on cognition expressed in linguistic categories. In Kinship analysis, he searched to classify cognitively contrasting components of specific kinship system. The most successful method is componential analysis method.

The componential analysis method avoids the use of ethnocentric kinship system, for instance uncle or cousin. It is because the relatives whom we call uncle may be classified quite differently elsewhere. Here all kinship terms are classified interms of distinctions such as age, sex, lineality, colaterality, generation, affinity, marital status, marital place and other culturally appropriate criteria. It results in a diagram which shows the formal cognitive roles in a kinship system, as it is utilised by the member of the group. In this way a researcher discovers what is going on inside some one's head, whether or not this proces is conscious. By interviewing native informants in the manner of anthropological linguists, who ulter contrasting sounds and then ask informants whether the contrasts are meaningful, the componential analysts produce cultural grammers or maps of semantic domain.

Colby (1996) has opined that core of ethno-science practiced in 1950s and 1960s was decision models and narrative grammers. These were added to the agenda of cognitive anthropology in 1970s. Discourse Semantics, concensus making and application of artificial were added in 1980 in cognitive anthropology. In 1990s theoriees of emotions, interest, health, well-being, religious symbolism and computer added discourse analysis came under it.

In 1980s, Schema theory was added in cognitive anthropology. It was related to the understanding of Psychological aspect of culture. Schemas as abstract entities are enacted unconsciously by individuals. They are models of world which organise experience and understanding shared by members of a group. For example writing. The schema of writing of a teacher, child, a cartoonist, and so on differs. But there is a common cultural notion of writing.

Consensus theory has also been added in cognitive anthropology. It addresses issues of reliability in data. It deals with not informations gathered, but the informants interviewed. It adds a researcher to describe and measure the extent to which cultural beliefs are shared.

Cognitive anthropology has established a bridge between culture and functioning of mind. It gives us an understanding as to how people order and perceive the world around. It helps us in understanding what is going on in someone's head.

5
Symbolic Anthropology

Introduction

The anthropological school which supports the view that social solidarity is a function of systems of logic that connect the people, especially during ritual is known as symbolic anthropology. Symbolic anthropology is also known as symbolism. The founder of this school is Victor Turner, a British anthropologist. Symbolic anthropology shares the same basic idea that culture is a Psychological or mental phenomena like ethno-science, ethno-linguistics, and cognitive anthropology. But it is different from them in several ways. Unlike ethno-science, ethno-linguistics and cognitive anthropology symbolic anthropology believes that symbols are external expressions of meaning and are not locked inside the head. The main focus of symbolic anthropology is studying the ways in which people understand their surroundings. It also takes into consideration the actions and utterances of other members of their society.

In the United States Max Weber was rediscovered by anthropologists in 1960s and 1970s. The rediscovery of Weber reflected and stimulated a new concern for importance of meaning and human potentiality to act creatively in the world. The fresh interests in exploring meaning was expressed in language of symbols.

The roots of symbolic anthropology in Britain and interpretive anthropology in United States can be traced back to the Neo Kantian philsophy of Wilhelm Dilthey and others had helped to formulate the distinction between the natural sciences and social sciences. According to this distinction promulgated by Franz Boas, natural sciences deal with entities amenable to generalisation, while social sciences deal with mental entities unique to individuals and groups. To this distinction phenomenologist-philosopher Edmand Husserl added his observation that natural science is unsuitable for the study of cultural life because cultural life has meaning which can be best understood subjectively as lived experience.

The classical interpretive and symbolic anthropologists were inspired by sound empirical research in the best anthropological tradition. They differed from their colleagues working in materialist and ecological traditions. According to symbolic anthropology and interpretive anthropologists, social and cultural worlds are held together by interpenetrating networks of symbols; each of which is a carrier of cultural meaning. The symbolists and interpretivists have this much in common. But inspite of this undealying similarity, the two schools differ profoundly. Symbolic anthropology has deep impact on the character of British Anthropology, whereas interpretative anthropology has a deep impact on character of American anthropology.

Contribution of Victor Turner (1920-1983) Victor Turner was the most influential and academically respected symbolic anthropologist in Great Britain. Like most anthropologists of his generation Victor Turner was heavily influenced by Emile Durkheim's concept that Social Solidarity or cohesion was achieved organically through the interpenetration of a given society's component parts. Moving beyond the previous generation of structural functionalist, for whom the essence of organic solidarity lays in the concrete institutions and formalise relations of society. Turner made focus on the Durkheimian idea that solidarity is a function of systems of symbolic logic that connect people. On the ground symbolic anthropology has much in common with Levi-Strauss' structuralism. But unlike his French Peers, for whom symbolic contrast and correspondences are seen as universal mental template on which all cultures are built. But according to Turner social unity is basically problematic. It can not be taken for granted. People are forced to repeatedly construct social life against those forces in natural world which constantly threaten to destory it. Since symbols are primary vehicles by which social solidarity is organised. They are tools or instruments employed by people to achieve a particular end the reproduction of social order.

Besides Durkheimain theory, Victor Turner was also credited to the ideas of Arnold Van Gennep, who had speculated about the ritual process in his book, *Rites of Passage* (1959). According to Van Gennep, rituals involves the passage of individuals from one social state to another The ritual entacts at three stages, seperation from the group, transition to a new state and incorporation within the social order. Turner elaborated his concept of ritual to include a theory of process based on Van Gennep's concept of liminality. Liminal is an ephemeral Psycho-social space in which social roles and arrangements are subject to transformation, inversion and affirmation. Turner believed that rituals generate a liminal period in which all notions of social structure are undone and a period of anti-structure ensues. This is what one can observe at time of carnival and varieties of initiation rites. The ritualised chaos of anti-structure involves inverting normal identities and roles. For examples men are ritually transformed into women, kings into servants and so on. Such anti-structure is possible because liminal state is one in which all limitations of everyday structure are dispensed with and new creative possibilities came into existence. Throughout all inverson and liminal transformation of norms and identities, members of a society ultimately come to recognize and reaffirm the basic structural cohesion that they had known all along, in their routine existence out side of ritual. This is the central aspect of this theory. By way of this new formed solidarity society avoids the truly revolutionary inapplications of liminal process and instead is fused in Communitas. According to Turner Communitas refer to the ritual fusion of individuals in to a collective identity.

Concept of Social Drama: While discussing symbolic anthropology, Victor Turner has talked about social drama. A social drama is a spontaneous unit of social process and a fact in everyone's experience in every society. Social drama can be broken in to four acts:

- ***Breach***—a rupture in social relation.
- ***Crisis***—that cannot be handled by normal strategies.
- ***Redress***—a remedy to the initial problem.
- ***Reintegration***—return to the *status quo* or an alternation in social arrangement.

6
Interpretive Anthropology

Introduction

The Anthropological school supporting the view that culture is lived experience integrated in a coherent public system of symbols that rendere the world intelligible is known as interpretive anthropology. This school was established by Clifford Greetz, an American anthropologist in United States. Clifford Greetz developed his own Semiotic theory of culture. Semiotic is pertaining to the relationship between symbols and what they represent. Semiotic theory of culture is also dependent on the social circulation and ritual performance of symbols.

The major differences between symbolic anthropology and interpretive anthropology are as follows:

- The founder of symbolic anthropology, Victor Turner was influenced by Emile Durkheim, whereas founder of interpretive anthropology, Clifford Greetz was influenced by Max Weber.
- Turner was concerned with the operation of society and the ways in which symbols operate within it, whereas Greetz was concerned with operation of culture and not with ways in which symbols operate in social process.
- Greetz has treated symbols as vechicle of culture, but Turner has treated symbols as operator in social process.
- Emphasis on meaning as opposed to structure has given Greetz's work a different orientation from his British counter part Turner.

Taking his clues from Boasian anthropologist Clyde, Klukhhohn Greetz's theory incorportes the idea that at the core of culture is a set of integrated moral values that preserve the correspondence of the world as it is with the world as it should be. As an interpretive anthropolist he showed that lived experiene is integrated in a coherent public system of symbols that renders the world intelligeble and seems uniquely suited to do so. According to him, the task of interpretive anthropology is to explore the ways in which symbols operate within culture.

Greetz was of opinion that analysis of culture should not be made as an experimental science in search of law, but it should be made as an interpretive one in search of meaning. Culture is expressed by external symbols that a society uses, rather than being locked inside people's head. According to him, culture is historically transmitted patterns of meaning embodied in people. It is a pattern by which men communicate, perpetuate and develop knowledge and attitude towards life. Societies use symbols to express their edos-world views, values, ethos or spiritual character and other cultural traits. Symbols play significant role in shaping their behaviour.

In his book, *Interpretation of Culture* (1973), Greetz has talked about thick discription technique for the interpretation of culture. According to him it is best ethnographic technique to interprete the text of culture. It deals with five details of human life that make their behaviour intelligible. For Greetz man is an animal suspended in webs of significance that he himself has spun. The interpretive anthropologists study culture not for discovering laws, but for searching meaning. The meaning not locked in the psychologies of individuals, but a network of significations that are on public display. This is particularly the case during rituals like the Balanise cock fight. In cock fight the social order of Balanise society lurks below the level of awareness embodied in symbols. It is collectively shared by all witness to the event.

To illustrate thick description technique, Greetz has cited an example, which discusses the difference between "blink" and "wink". Blink is involuntary twitch in eye, whereas Wink is a signal to a friend. Blink is their thin description, whereas Wink is thick description. In both situations, the movement of eyelids are concerned and they are identical. But they have different meaning. A Wink is a special form of communication which is deliberated to someone in particular, to impart a particular message. It has a socially established code, without the knowledge of other members of group of which Winkater and Winky are parts. The combination of Blink and Winks produce a stratified hierarchy of meaningful structures. The object of ethnography is to decipher such hierarchy of cultural categories.

INTERPRETIVE PERSPECTIVE IN ARCHAEOLOGY

The interpretive perspective in archaeology came into existence in 1980s when some archaeologists became disenchanated with the New archaeology of Binford. New archaeology had adhrence to Cartesian rationalism and objectivity. They were not ready to accept the significance of nomothetic or scientific approach of Lewis Binford. According to them, archaeology was more closely allied to history than to science. As history was a humanity, the holistic explanation of Boasian particularism seemed more appropriate than covering law model and economic determinism of Lewis Binford. Some of these archaeologists embranced the view point of critical anthropologists that science is elitist. They also accepted the view of French structuralist and structural Marxists that material culture has a symbolic dimension, consciousness causes change and artifacts reveal social relation as well as adaptation to invironment.

In mid-1980s, British archaeologist, Ian Hodder codified these views in to what he called contextual or post-processual archoeology. According to contextual or post-processual archaeologist, artifacts are embedded into a web of cultural discourse that affirms social relations and enhances the power of previledged groups. Post-processualists were of view that quest to discover law like process of culture change, the characterstics of New archaeology should be abandoned. Like symbolists and post-modernist in anthropology, post-processualist in archaeology criticised the pure scientific objectivity as unattainable and undesirable theoretical goal.

Symbolic and interpretive approaches during 1960s and 1970s had criticised the authorative knowledge in anthropology at least in cynical environment of late twentieth century academy. The same cynicism that cultivated the particularistic, Neo Kantian tendencies in 1960s and 1970s also gave rise to political economy in mid-1970s.

The political economy opposes symbolic and interpretive anthropology in its renewal emphasis on history and objectivity. It was not the structuralism of British and French, but a new body of thought inspired heavily by the historicism of Marx and Engels. According to political economists, cultures are not merely local, trans-local and are shaped by unequal access to power and material resources. Symbolic and interpretive anthropologists were criticised not because they laid too much emphasis on meaning. But because they do away with the notion of structure. Political economists insisted on a new structural orthodoxy in which individual agency still had no real place and in which social change could not be really accomodated.

PHENOMENOLOGICAL ANTHROPOLOGY

The school of anthropology which supports the study of culture as a way of doing ethnography and ethnologoy emphasizing the human feelings and consciousness, is known as phenomeno logical anthropology.

The root of phenomenological anthropology can be traced back to Neo-Kantian philosophy of Wilhelm Dilthey and others. They had formulated a distinction between natural science and social science. Following this distinction Franz Boas had promulgated that natural sciences deal with entities amenable to generalisations, while social sciences deal with mental entities unique to individual and groups.

To the above distinction, phenomenological philosopher Edmund Husserl had added his observation that natural science was unsuitable for the study of cultural life. It is because cultural life has a meaning which can be best understood subjectively as lived experience.

Being influenced by phenomenological philosopher, phenomenological anthropologists attempted to do ethnographic fieldwork and ethnological studies subjectively as lived experience or consciousness. Phenomenological anthropology is concerned with methods that can be employed in fieldwork to get in to the native's head and understand what the native is experiencing. This can be done subjectively as lieved experence. We can make phenomenological study of hand-shake, clapping, whistling, shoulder to shoulder meet, chest to chest meet, kissing, eyemovement, tongue movement, sitting arrangement in class, serving feast, performing ritual, identifying diseases, curing diseases, literacy behaviour, health behaviour, fertility behaviour and so on. Infanct a phenomenological anthropological study is one which is grounded in direct experience of one's own consciousness.

Phenomenological anthropology has recognised that non-Euro-American cultures have produced their own phenomenology and techniques. One of the most renowed phenomenologists for ethnographic fieldworks was Paul Recoeur. He had made argument against structuralist method of Claude Levi-Strauss. Levi-strauss had expressed view that text could be interpreted independently without actual experiences of the people who told the myth. Ricoeur made a counter argument that an acurate interpretation of native's text could not be made independently without the actual experience of the living people who were influenced by the text. In other word it can be said that true hermeneutics involves a dialogue between a text (myth, drama, and history, story and legends) and experiences evoked in people participating in the text. Thus, in phenomenological study meaning of the text is developed within the consciousness of living people. The real meaning of the text is grounded by direct experience of people and their consciousness.

The emergence of phenomenological anthropology has allowed the issue of experience, feeling and consciousness in the scientific discourse which were excluded since long period. It has reintroduced the ethnographic fieldwork and to build ethnological theory. It has brought to the light the social grounded theory and true hermeneutic theory for doing ethnography and ethnology.

7
Critical Anthropology (Political Economy)

Introduction

A critical school of thought had emerged in socio-cultural anthropology in 1970s. This critical school of thought is also known as political economy. The political economist were critical of symbolic and interpretive anthropology. They have placed emphasis on history and objectivity. This was not like old structuralism of British and French. It was a new body of thought inspired by the historicism of Marx and Engels. The political economists were of view that cultures are not only local, but also translocal. They are shaped and directed by unequal possession of power and material resources.

Right from the early 1950, anthropologists were feeling less and less comfortable with the idea that anthropologist must study pristine, self-contained and largely rural communities. In particular, Rober Redfield developoed a theoretical distinction between the great tradition of lite rate, religious and urban in contrast to little tradition of illiterate, magical and rural. But the connection between the developed and underdeveloped world remained largely under-theorised until about a decade later.

The origin of political economy can be traced to the writing of influential economist Andre Gunder Frank. He began to criticise the agenda of moderisation in 1960s. He was of opinion that global capitalist agenda was more sinister than benign. It had made those nation-states satellite dependent with which western world came in into contact. The Western world had extracted surplus goods and labour in exchange of satellites on very less payment. According to him underdevelopment was not a product of local condition, but the result of progressive capitalist exploitation.

The historian Immanuel Wallerstein (1974) also identified a historical emergence of Euro-American world economy. In this economy bourgeois capitalist in the core nations of Europe and America appropriate the profits generated by proletarians in the perephery. Wallerstein also like Frank found proletariate trapped in a world system of unequal exchange. The Euro-American society had penetrated, politically subjugated and economically exploited the external people and their produce. Thus, the concept of political economy came in to existence.

The emergence of political economy paved the ways for emancipatory social movements such as counter culture, antiwar, anti-colonial and feminiest movement on a large scale in Western society. The philosophical foundation of these movements were based in the academic world itself. It had brought a marked influence on the intellectual discourse for socio-cultural anthropology, it was a period of introspection. It was quite clear that the discipline of anthropology had failed to deal with the impact of colonial and imperialism around the world. It could not recognise the essential links between rise of anthropological knowledge and colonial encounter.

All classical ethnographics were written by White Euro-American men. Their work was made possible by political and military subjugation of the people whom they studied. According to political economists, the remote and exotic communities of classic ethnographies were captive and dependent on a global system of capitalism and militarism. Anthropologists come to understand the fault of their discipline. They were profitted by opression of the communities whom they had described in sympathetic manner. Now, many basic assumptions and truth value of anthropological knowledge were criticised from various quarters. The most severe criticism was the pristine, timeless and self-contained organic communities of anthropological inquiry. These concepts were criticised as figment of the ethnographic imagination. The empirical research of ethnography was also brought under question. The authors of ethnographies were criticised as impartial or objective.

Now, a number of scholars begain to display, rather than canceal or mystify, various conflincts such as class interests, arrangements of power and dependently embedded in the history of global Capitalism. It was a history in which anthropology had also played a role. It was out of this post-structural concern for social process, power, conflict and the origin of authorative knowledge, the political economy had came in to existence. In anthropology, post-structural is an adjective that expresses disenchantment with static, mechanistc and controlling model of society and culture and a consequent interest in social process and agency. Authorative knowledge is the idea that one body of knowledge and understanding is previledged over other bodies, in that it has greater acess to ultimate reality or the truth.

KARL MARX

According to political economy, culture has been shaped within the context of unequal access to wealth and power. The school of political economy or critical anthropology, was deeply influenced by the writings of the Karl Marx. This school may be thought as materialist, because the material conditions of human existence are understood to condition the character of social relations. They were influenced by cultural materialists who viewed infrastructure (mode of production and mode of reproduction) as a primary determinant of culture. They embraced Marxian ideology. The term ideology was employed by Karl Marx and his supporters to denote a system of beliefs that knowingly or unknowingly influences the perspectives and out looks of individuals and groups. According to Marxian ideology whoever controls the means of producing wealth and power, also controls the conditions for production of knowledge. When the knowledge about the world is taken for guaranted, it losses its arbitrary character and is seen as natural. At this stage, the ideolgoy becomes a dominent perspectives of the society. It is taken for granted by powerful and powerless alike. Unchallenged dominant ideologies, such as cluster of heterogeneous meanings and activities that make up global capitalism, recapituate the economic and political interests of some, while mystifying this essential inequality in power relations for other the political economists refer to this mystification as hegemony. It refers to the capacity of one social group to impose particular belief or political and economic conditions upon another group.

There is no doubt that in the hand of political economy the concept of culture has been reconceived. Now, in-place of immaterial and meta-physical concept of culture, culture became a system of objective and concrete forces or ideologies. Now, culture was not perceived as unified and undifferentiated object of study. Some recent generation theoreticians have treated culture as problematic. They have raised a question under what social and historical conditions particular interests and activities come into existence?, how do they create new meanings and practices? and how are they received, accepted, modified and resisted ? By answering such questions anthropologists have moved their discipline from traditional communities study. While community study viewed culture as timeless, exotic and autonomous. Now, anthropologists started in 1970s and 1980s to study the impact of penetration of large scale regional, national and international political economic forces on local societies. They started studying the influence of global political economy on local communities. Sidney Minzeb (1986), William Roseberry (1989) and Ericwolf (1982) are known as prominent political economist anthropolists who have contributed to illuminate these issues over the post-quarter century.

Undoubtedly, the efforts brought by political economist anthropologists to understand the penetration of global and local forces have shown the changing and malleable character of cultures, but it has also raised a number of questions for answer by some other scholars. If ethnographic texts of exotic timeless, other prepared by early generation anthropologists did not reflect objective reality, how it was possible to liberate themselves to new generation cultural anthropologists from ethnocentrism. The timeless other cultures were still very different from Euro-American cultures. Political economy is also ethnocentric because it insists that culture is product of material power struggle uniquely. Anthropologists began to think whether it was desirable to continue to seek any one causes or configuration of causes that determine culture, may be historical, colonial, industrial and scientific progress. These questions are significant because they cut the very heart of what anthropology attempts to do. Anthropologists devise a powerful and parsimonious models which explain as to how people interact with each other and the world. Most cultural anthropologists came to realise for extracting the anthropology from its modernist heritage. Modernist heritage devides world into Cartesian oppositions subject-object, self other, rational-irrational, material-ideal and nature-culture. It is very difficult to prove these oppositions.

8
Modernism

Introduction

The school of Anthropological thought which deals with the impact and consequences of enlightment, scientific revolution, industrial revolution, capitalism, democracy, secularisaton and modern education is known as school of modernism. The scholars belonging to this school are known as modernists and their theory is known as modernism. Karl Marx, Durkheim, Max Weber, Talcot Parsons, Ulrich Beck, George Ritzer, Zygmunt Bauman, Peter Hamilton, Lyotar and Jurgen Habermas are scholars of this school.

ORIGIN OF MODERNISM

There was a time when religion was regarded as all kinds of events—good and bad in the world. Even human beings were made sacrifice in the name of Gods and Goddesses. Tradition and state religion were interrelated. Thereafter, enlightment came. The emergence of enlightment made the traditions ill. The period of eighteenth Century intellectual history preceding the French revolution is known as enlightment. Many traditions were rejected on the basis of facts and logic. Blinds faith were rejected on the basis of truth. Attempts were made to understand events on the basis of knowledge. In this way with the emergence of enlightment modernity and modernism came into existence. It is a matter between eighteenth and nineteenth Century. Now, Feudalism replaced capitalism. Scientific revolution gave rise to industriality and which ultimately gave rise to capitalism, democracy and secularism. Now social relation got national and international ground. Concept of consumerism and marketism were developed. Imperialism came into existence and politics of power got success all over the world. Now imperialism and economic competition became interrelated. Villages developed into towns, town developed into cities and cities developed into metropolises.

Some Definitions of Modernism

There is no doubt that modernism is a historical process. But it is related to ideology and some values. According to George Ritzer, modernism is not only a historical process, but it is deeply related to ideology and save values. Previously religion held strong hold in the society, but now secular values have been added in the society. This, transformation of traditional society into modern society is modernism. Modernism is ideology-oriented and value-oriented.

Modernism may also be defined as a special type of culture termed as plural culture or multicultural. In modernism, social, economic and political systems are closely linked. Due to this interrelationship a special plural culture is formed. This plural culture includes cultures of different ethnic groups, religious groups, regional groups and lingual groups. In this way modernism is a flexible concept.

British sociologists, Anthony Giddens in his book, *The Consequences of Modernity* (1990) has defined modernism interms of four basic institutions which are as follows:

- Capitalism
- Industrialism
- Administrative Power
- Nation-State

Thus, according to Anthony Giddens, modernism is sum total of four institutions—capitalism, industrialism, administrative power and nation-state.

Anthony Giddens has further added two more characteristics of modernism which are as follows:

- Reflex Society
- Disembeded Society

Anthony Giddens was of opinion that modern society is a reflex society. Now, the concept of time and distance both have received a new definition. Time boundary and distance boundary have been so contracted that people have relationship with the speed of electricity. It takes few seconds to talk anywhere in the word through the means of communication system. Now, the world is in the hand through cell phones and internet. The most importand feature of the modernism is that its reflect is found in all societies. All wives residing in different communities of all world have come to know about divorce, divorce rule, compensation. All ethnic groups have come to know their human rights.

Giddens has also talked about disembded society. It is also closely related to time and place. We do not find the concept of community life. In traditional society community members used to lead a collective life. They shared joys and sorrows together. But modern society joys and sorrows have become a personal life concern.

American Scholar Talcott Parsons has defined modernism as a bundle of values. It is related to specialisation. More modern societies have more specialisation. He developed the concept of patten variable. He was of opinion that before doing any work a situation of uncertainty comes in to existence. Before doing a work an individual behaves according to his tradition. He takes decision according to his value. What should be done or what should not be done. Pattern variable makes a society traditional or modern.

According to Parsons, a modern society is one which has values of emotional impartiality, speciality, achievement and collectivity.

Ulrich Beck has attempted to define modernism in some what different ways. According to him the culture of modernism has a culture of danger. The classical modernism was industrial modernism. But the present day modernism is of danger which is different from nineteenth century modernism. In modern modernism one finds more individualisation. This individual is out of control. This individual does not behave according to his caste, religion, language and region. He behaves above them. Such individuals are danger for the society. They have more and more money. The industrialists, traders, and merchants are influencing negatively in their society. Thus, such a dangerous society has emerged which has created threat to generations to come. The modernism in which we are leading our life today, is politicalisation of nature. The ughy scene of industrialisation and pollution is dangerous and against our existence.

George Ritzer has attempted to define modernism on the basis of concept of rationality propounded by Karl Marx and Max Weber. Max Weber had propounded the concept of rationalism on the basis of study of religion and power. According to him modernism is a rational concept. He had examined the concept of rationality at the structural level. According to him bureaucracy is a rational structure. Similarly, religion is also a formal rational structure. Both bureaucracy and religion have been able to provide special place to their rational. Rational has different formal types which are available to us. Ritzer has pushed forward the concept of rationality propounded by Weber. He cited the examples of fast food restaurant and credit card. Both functions on the basis of rationality. Similarly, Americanisation is also a formal rationale. It has a solid economic rationale. These are examples of modernism. In this way Ritzer has defined modernism as developed rationale.

Zygmunt Bauman has presented a very ugly picture of modernism. According to him, structural formal rationale sometimes pushes towards destruction. For example killing of thousand jews in Second World War by Naziz in gas chamber of Germany. Similarly, the attack on New York and Washington on 11.09.2001 was also an example of rational destruction. Bauman was of opinion that bureaucracy is not impartial. It is like a loaded gun which can be used in the direction in which power wants. Here, attention is not paid on value of human life and property. Here, attention is paid on the fulfilment of political ends.

From the above account it is clear that modernism is related to intellect and rationale. It is closely related to democracy, capitalism and industiralism. But now-a-day, it is explained as an intellectual act of fast food restaurant, credit card and destruction. Modernism is a very broad concept. There is no one modernism in the world. The world is an example of plural modernism.

Chief Characteristics of Modernism

On the basis of above definitions provided by different classical and modern scholars, modernism has the following chief characteristics:

- Modernism is universal phenomenon
- Modernism originated in nineteenth Century
- Modernism is result of evolution
- Modernism originated as a national and international process.
- Modernism is related to capitalism, industrialism and secularism.
- Modernism has different styles of life
- Modernism is a power of social relation and conflict.
- Modernism is full of danger.
- Modernism is competitive.
- Modernism has individualisation.
- Modernism is a rationale concept.
- Modernism is related to destruction.
- Globalisation, privatisation and liberalisation are brethren of modernism.

Theories of Modernism

There is a debate on theories of modernism among the scholars. Theoreticians are of opinion that contemporary society is a modern society. Contemporary society has capitalism, industrial revolution and rationality. Against this theory there is opinion that modern society has come to an end and post-modern society has come in to existence. Some main theories related to modernism are as follows:

- Enlightment Theory of Modernism
- Tradition-Modernism Continuum Theory
- Weber's Theory of Modernism
- George Simmel's Theory of Modernism
- Contemporary Theory of Modernism

Enlightment Theory of Modernism

According to this theory proper explanation of modernism can be made with the help of enlightment theory. Enlightment is a historical event. This event has given birth to modernism. The intellectual history of Europe is known as enlightment. Its period has been from 1689-1789. In the year 1689 the book of Issac Newton entitled,

Principle of Mathematics was published. In the year 1789, French revolution was initiated. The publication of Newton's book had brought a revolution in traditional society of Europe. Newton had expressed distrust towards the religion. He was of opinion that the only way to reach the truth is science. Objectivity is the source of knowledge. As a result people began to express distrust in traditional truth. Infact the period of enlightment was the period of scienctific revolution in which intellectual attainments were made by different scholars in Europe.

A contemporary thinker of Newton John Locke (1689) supported the human understanding to know the society. At the same time Russo, Montesque, Walbir and David Hume in France propounded their theories. The book of Adam Smith entitled, *The Wealth of Nation* was published. Smith propounded his theory that the behaviour of man in market is rationale or logical. He thinks of maximum profit before buying or utilising things. He was also of opinion an that more division of labour was related to more production.

The central philosophy of enlightment theory was logic. This logic was related to every aspects. This brought a change in science and social science in looking at the society. A new activity was also initiated in philosophy. Expressinig his opinion German philosopher Immanual Kant said that place and time are nothing in themselves. Whatever meaning man provides to them, they assume the same meaning. Both are subjective objects not same as they appear. Rather understanding of objects as they are seen is science. This is true.

During the period of enlightment man was forced to think about the source of origin of knowledge. The philosophy of knowledge was main topic of enlightment period. The main point here was that how we know the object and what we know about the object. This entire area was of philosophy. On one hand, emphasis was placed on logic or rationalism and on emptricism on the other hand. Both traditions had their own supporters and opponents. This debate was responsible for the origin of modernism. The supporters of enlightment theory are of opinion that the base of modernism is logic, knowledge, impiricity and science. The concept of culture in anthropology is also a gift of enlightment.

Peter Hamilton was of opinion that the modernism attained a real definition in enlightment period. It was possible through scientific and ideological revolution. Enlightment is true theory for the analysis of modernism. This theory has following features:

- ***Logic***: Modernism is a rationale behaviour in the context.
- ***Empiricity***: This behaviour is logical and empirial.
- ***Science***: Modernism is based on science.
- ***Universality***: Modernism is a universal phenomenon.
- ***Progress***: Modernism is related to progress.
- ***Individualism***: Modernism is individualistic.
- ***Liberality***: Modernism is related to liberalism.
- ***Freedom***: Modernism is related to freedom.
- ***Uniformity in Nature of Man***: Enlightment has brought uniformity in the nature of man.
- ***Secularism***: Modernism is related to secularism.

Criticism: The enlighment theory of modernism has been subjected to criticism. Jean Francisco Lyotard has criticised this theory because this theory has provided the occasion of exploitation of lower class by upper class.

Some scholars have criticised this theory on the ground that it has initiated conflict between tradition and modernism. Enlightment theory has nourished the conflict between traditionalism and modernism.

The idea of progress based on Marxism in Enlightment is also not acceptable. Now, we have a concept of mass society. In this society pre-ideological devisions have no importance and the freedom of individual is against objective social relations.

But inspite of all these critcism, enlightment theory is regarded as a successful theory. It is because this theory was able to free itself from the God. The philosopher of this period were of view that creation may be a boon of God, but society is man made. In the building of society, God has no place. It has developed the concept of logic which is only alternative to search for truth. It was for the first time that material objects were seperated from the mind. Enlightment established for the first time the concept of a rational individual. Now, individual occupied significant place in social relations in place of God and spirituality.

Tradition-modernism Continuum Theory

Towards the end of nineteenth century Ferdenand Toyneese had attempted to understand the concept of modernism on the basis of tradition-modernism continuum. According to him traditionism and modernism developed in two historical periods in two situations, but they were not in isolation. They were interdependent and interrelated. Both are complements to each other. They show continuum. There is modernism in traditionism and traditionism in modernism.

After the down ball of Feudalism, the traditionism had become strong. A strong inseperable relation was formed between state and religion. States were run by churches. But after the invention of science the influence of religion was weakened. Now, the thinking of people became logical and realistic. Steam engine was invented in this period. This provided the momentum to industrial revolution. Industries were estalished in entire Europe and America and cottage industries met an end. The First World War was started in this period. A large number of people migrated to urban areas from their villages. This was a historical event. This event gave a halt to traditionism and an occasion to emerge the modernism. Previously tradition used to unite the people. But now unity was brought by modernism.

In order to make a distinction between traditionism and modernism, Toyneese developed the concept of Gemeinschaft and Gesellschaft. On the basis of these concepts he showed that urbanisation and industrialisation pushed the human communication forward from traditionism to modernism. His concept of Gemeinschaft was related to traditional community and Gesellschaft was related to modern society.

According to him the traditional community has following features:

- Small size
- Fixed population
- Birth based status
- Family, kinship and religion has special place
- Special place for traditional values
- Sentimental expressions
- Tribal and peasant society

According to Toyneese traditional society was pre-industrial society. But modernism made its approach to traditional society through industrialisation, urbanisation and secularisation. The modern society has following characteristic:

- Complex division of labour
- Impersonal relation
- Non-sentimental relation
- Formal relation
- Importance of competition
- Class based society
- Large population
- Elite class
- Importance of modern value
- Importance of achieved status

Durkheim's Theory of Modernism

Emile Durkheim in his book, *Division of Labour in Society* (1893) has talked about mechanical solidarity and organic solidarity. According to him, mechanical solidarity is characteristic of traditional society and organic solidarity is characteristc of modern society. He has attempted to present an evolutionary view of modernism. Modernism has evolved from traditionalism. Organic solidarity was an integration of similarity. There was lack of stratification in it. People were integrarted collectively. There was a we feeling and people were united by common sentiments. They used to share the same value system. There was homogeneity. This was characteristic features of traditional or pre-industrial society.

According to Durkheim, mechanical society changed in to organic society with the process of industrialisation and mechinisation. Now, simple mechanical society was transformed in to a complex organic society. In this society the division of labour was not based on age and sex: Rather the division of society was based on ability and speciality. Now expert, creative and rationale individuals came in to existence. Specialisation of labour brought stratification in society. Now, solidarity was maintained by complex division of labour, stratification, expertise, ability, class system and density of population.

They do not hamper integration, rather they maintain integration in the society.

Max Weber's Theory of Modernism

Famous German theoretician Max Weber has propounded the theory of modernism on the basis of freedom. According to him, logic and rationale have played significant role in freeing man from the tradition. Modernism has emerged due to logic, rationality and creativity. He presented such a model of modernism which was based on bureaucracy and creativity. As rationality went on increasing, man became more and more free from the traditionism. The following are the chief characteristics of modernism.

- Scientific truth
- Capitalism
- Marketism
- Class stratification
- Creativity, logic and rationality
- Political ideology

Weber had attempted to deal his theory of modernism on the basic of religion. He was of opinion that Calvinism of Christianity had supported the capitalism. In this way religion had also extended its support to modernism and capitalism.

Weber's theory of modernism can be understood in the context of theory of Karl Marx. Marx and Weber both had explained the theory of modernism in the context of capitalism, but their approaches were different. Marx had placed his emphasis on means of production. According to him, middle class was owner of means of production. Productive powers remain in their hands. Labour class sells its labour. But Weber has explained the capitalism in the context of market. According to him, the market provides a number of occasion in the life of man through capitalism. These occasions shared by both rich and poor. Class is different from the market. Class has age, ability and skill. In this way, Weber has opined clearly that modernism is a gift of rationality and capitalism.

George Simmel's Theory of Modernism

Simmel has explained the concept of modernism on the basis of urban centres and money. In his famous book, '*Philosophy of Money*', he has discussed the relation between modernism and money in the following ways:

- Money is a means for the fulfilment of different kinds of needs. It makes man powerful. He termed this power as epiphany.
- Money forced the Feudal society to transform itself into capitalist society. Now, people became pleased. But it also gave birth to seperatist tendency. In capitalist system individual remains cut off from the mainstream.
- Money has created two kinds of culture which are as follows:
- Tragedy culture
- Objective culture

Tragedy culture is result of seperatist tendency, whereas objective culture is culture of few people who lead a pleasant life.

- Due to industrialisation concentration of money is found in cities. Modernism gradually moves from cities to villages.

Contemporary Theory of Modernism

American and European society of to-day is not a society of eighteenth century. Now, their forms have changed. The present day society has new economic system. Globalisation has emerged as a new power. The concept of time and place have became narrow and have changed due to space technology. The classical theories of modernism propounded by Karl Marx, Durkheim, Weber, Simmel and Toyneese is no more significant. They have become irrelevant. The challenges brought by post-modernism has put a question on the existence of modernism. But some contemporary theories are facing challenges of post-modernism bravely. We are going here to deal with only those contemporary theory.

George Ritzer's Theory of Modernism

George Ritzer was one of contemporary theoretician(s) of modernism. He presented the concept of rationality developed by Weber in modified form. According to Ritzer ratonality, intellect and logic are of different forms. For example Americanisation, McDonaldisation and fast food fashion are different forms of rational. Thus, he has presented modernism thorugh Americanisation, McDonaldisation and Hyperrationality. For him, rationality is key of modernism.

Hyperrationality: It is the chief feature of modern society. Max Weber had classified rationality in to following four types:

- Formal rationality
- Real rationality
- Theoretical rationality
- Behavioural rationality

Formal rationality: Formal rationality includes the structures of bureaucracy and leadership action. In different structures the actions of individuals are different. They receive their ends through different means. The means and end has logical relation.

Real rationality: In real rationality there is dominance of norms and values. Here, individual achieves means and ends through norms and value.

Theoretical rationalism: In theoretical rationality, individual uses rational cognitive processes and tries to achieve ends on that basis.

Behavioural rationality: In this type of rationality means ends are selected on the basis of daily actions.

Out of all four types of rationality, Weber regards formal rationality as key of modernism.

Ritzer has added the concept of hyperrationality in the concept of rationality propounded by Weber. In the situation of hyper-rationality all four forms are integrated. He cited example of Japanese automobile as an example of hyperrationality.

In McDonaldisation Ritzer added formal structure of rationality. McDonald is a name of an American restaurant whose several branches are providing food services in different parts of the globe. It renders services of fast food to its customers quickly. Here rationality is found behind serving fast food to customer. Fast food has become a feature of modernism. McDonaldisation is an example of Hyperrationality.

Ritzer has attempted to discuss the concept of modernism through Americanisation. Americanisation is an example of Hyperrationality. Americanisation of all countries have taken place through fast food and credit card.

Jugren Habermass, Theory of Modernism

Jugren Habermass was a German Sociologist. Though he was a Marxist, but he had supported the capitalism. He was of opinion that capitalism has no alternative in present contex. Marx had pointed out two kinds of demerits related to capitalism. One demerit was related to recession and the other was related to exploitation and seperation. Habermass added public sector in it. He held view that orthodox democracy was not fruitful now-a-day. Therefore, public sector, should be added to it. Besides democratic organisations, we have also to depend upon public sector for arriving at a decision: In present day society transformations can be brought by making a change in public sectors. The role of communication agencies or media has increased now-a-day. But means of communications are not available equally everywhere.

In this way modernism is still under half scheme. We have to fulfil those weakness. Only then we can imagine about a post-modern society. The major parts of the world today are disabled and leading their life under tragedy. Without bringing them in mainstream, we cannot think of rationalism and modernism. Rationality is of no value for them who are still surviving for their existence. By bringing reform in the system, the project of modernism can be completed.

Ulrick Beck's Theory of Modernism

Ulrick Beck has attempted to explain the theory of modernism on the basis of risk. There is no doubt that prosperity in present day society has been brought by rationality and capitalism; but it has also induced risk in the society. The risk has various dimensions. In modern society some people are leading their life with all comforts, but majority of people are leading their life under tragedy. Capitalism and industrialisation have been able to produce goods on large scale. But they are also responsible for emergence of slums. The problem of pollution also comes into existence. A number of dangerous diseases have also made their deep root in the society. Thus, modern society is full of risk. This contemporary system of modernism is completely new. He was opponent of post-modernism. But he admitted that the modernism of to-day is under change. Now in place of industrial society, risk society has emerged. He has developed the concept of risk society in his book, *Risk Society* (1992). In this book he has attempted to show that modernism in its first phase has ended Feudal system and is ready to end industrial society in its second phase. According to Beck different types of risk are as follow:

- Manufactured Risk
- Health Risk
- Inequality Risk

***Manufactured Risk*:** Previously, we used to face natural risk like flood, femine, earthquake and epidemic risks. But now we are facing water pollution, air pollution, sound pollution, soil pollution risks. Rationality has put us under threat now. The machines we have made are our great enemy today.

***Health Risk*:** Technological and industrial development has gifted us some such dangerous diseases which are causing us death and we have no sufficient means to fight with them. Such diseases are AIDS, Cancer and heart diseases. Chemical fertiliser and pesticides have increased the productivity of foodgrains and vegetables, but they have given birth to a number of diseases in plants, animals and man.

***Inequality Risk*:** Today our modern societies are also facing the unequality risk. The capitalism has made us unequal socially culturally, economically and materially.

Beck has pointed out the dangers prevalent in our modern society. But he found post-modern society full of risks. Today industrial society is at death bed and modernism has reached into second phase. The modern society of to-day is *reflexive society*. In reflexive society individuals become free from traditions. In this society social relation is determined by individual not by society. Now, individuals decides to have relation, continue relation, break relation, follow which tradition, break which tradition and so on. Individualism is centre of reflexive society. The foundation of reflexive society is based on risks. This risk is above time and place.

The risk is not related to any one class. Rather it is related to all classes. For example the risk of pollution is above class. Although risk like wealth is also related to class. But this relation is opposite to wealth. Wealth is centred at upper level, risk is centred at lower level. Risk does not provide to abolish class system, but it provides strongness to the class system. That is why the poor have more efficiency to take risk. The rich who have more wealth, power and education do not like to take risk. He becomes free from risk by buying the risk. Like individual risk is also applicable to nation. The poor nation takes more and more risk and face the risk. The rich nation becomes free from the risks. The poor nations sell their technologies to poor nations. They store garbage in the sea areas of poor nations. They become free from the risk of pollution. But they are also not completely free from the danger of pollution, because the regions where machines manufacture are not free from pollution risk. It is possible that some face less risk and other face more risk. But all have to face risk and danger. The poor are more under the threat, and the rich are less under the threat. They become rich by selling risk. Thus, rationality of modern society is under the threat of risk and danger.

Zygmunt Bauman's Theory of Modernism

Zygmunt Bauman has attempted to explain his theory of modernism on the basis of destruction. According to him, the rationality of modern society lies in the destruction. Destruction is product of rationality. We finds the rationality of bureaucracy in the destruction. In this way modernism and destructionism have elective activity. Our history is a witness that whenever destruction and mass killing have been done, it was the hand of rationality of bureancracy. Destruction or killing is not an impulse or sentiment. It is a well thought and planned action of bureaucracy. Bauman has cited the example of Naziz of Germany during Second World War. They had made a plan to kill Jews and force them to go anywhere. Jews were thrown in gas chamber. This was not an act of cruel mentality, but well thought and planned action. Naziz made at cruel attack on Jews because Jews had rational industries. Thus, mdoernism is characterised by destruction.

Anthony Gidden's Theory of Modernism

Anthony Giddens has attempted to explain his theory of modernism on the basis of running society. The entire globe is in hand. The entire world is running here and there. The modern society has become running society due to risk. The entire world is engaged in sale and purchase of risks. Every nations are involved in this business. They are not getting stoppage anywhere.

Among all theories of Giddens, theory of modernism and theory of structuration are of great significane. We find the glims of his theories in his book, *Capitalism and Modern Social Theory* (1973) and, *Consequences of Modernity* (1990). According to Gidden modern society is running society because it is full of risk. In present modern society, capitalists are producing risks and selling those risks in hands of poor. The capitalists are leading luxurious life and the poor are leading risk full life. In this society, nobody has faith on other body. The entire world looks like stoppage among runners.

Giddens is a modernistic thinker: He has not linked modernism with liberalism and capitalism. He treats modernism as multi-dimensional concepts. The present day world is changing so fastly that classical theory of modernism has become irrelevant. It has become essential for contemporary theories to deal with those problems tactfully.

According to Giddens, factors for causing mobility in modern societies are as follows:

- Isolation of place and time
- Unembededness of social systems
- Reflexivity of modern society
- Institutional aspect of modernism
- Globalisation of modernism
- Post-traditional society

Isolation of Time and Place: In traditional society, time and place were together in society. But in modern society time and place have been isolated from the society. In traditional societies members lived together, worked together and shared joys and sorrows together. But in modern society the concepts of time and place has changed. Different members of the same family reside at different places and carryout different kinds of professions. They have their spread not only within the country, but also up to foreign countries. They live seperately, but are linked through modern means of communication and remain 24 hours in touch. They assemble on the occasion of death, marriage and birth functions, for few days or few hours and then they return their work places. Thus, time and place are now completely isolated from the society. Their standaradisation has taken place. All members of modern society accepts this standard gladly.

Unembededness of social systems: Modernism has brought the traditional society and social relation outside the boundary of locality. Now, they have been integrated to the wider world. The homogeneity of traditional society is vanishing. Homogenety has changed into heterogeneity. Now, village dwellers have also been integrated to the world through television, satellite, cellphone and internet. They have new news of all parts of the globe. The members of vilages are also found in towns, cities, metropolises and foreign countries.

According to Giddens heterogenety is of two types:

- Symbolic unembededness
- Specialist unembededness

He cited example of money as symbolic heterogeneity. Money funtions as symbol in modern society. Money symbols have influenced all types of societies—Folk, peasant and urban. Money has become a symbol of wealth. It has affected barter system and *Jajamani* system adversely. Now, payment is made and received in cash. Money symbol has become strong now-a-day. Now-a-day, symbol is work method of modern society. This has abolished the traditions and traitional value. Now-a-day, modern society performs its work through the medium of symbol.

The second work method of heterogeneity is system of experts or specialists. Its example is bank. The modern society has been built through the medium of specialists. We travel through bicycle, two wheeler, car, bus, railway and aeroplane. In making these vehicles, different specialists contribute their expertise. Ticket system and fare system are also result of experts.

In this way, localilty comes out of tradition through the medium of symbols and specialists or experts.

***Reflexivity of Modern Society*:** According to Giddens, the modern society has become reflexive society through mass communication system. In this society we find reflexivity. The members of modern society interact as per their individual needs; not as per will of the society. Mass communication system—cinema, T.V., cellphones, internet, books, Journals etc. makes the relation between individuals and society a complex phenomenon. There is no doubt, we have increased our knowledge, but it has made our behaviour reflexive. We begin to behave as per media of communication. Developed tele-communication system has made us orthodox.

***Institutional aspect of Modernism*:** According to Giddens modern society also has institutional aspects. Modern society is a vast network of institutions. Different institutions like social, economic, political, religious, cultural, educational and health institutions work in modern society. Institutions were present in traditional society too. They are also present in modern society. But the modern society has four institutional aspects which are as follows:

- Capitalism
- Industrialism
- Administrative Power
- Military Power

The modern society performs its functions through these four institutions, which are interdependent, interrelated and complements to each other. But these four institutions also give rise to movements. The movements bring new system into existence.

The capitalism gave rise to labour movement and socialistic economic organisations were built. The industrialism gave rise to ecological and cultural movement. Due to this movement sustainable system and forestry were introduced. Administrative system brought movements related to human rights and civil movements into existence. Because of these movements multi-level democratic system was built. Due to military power, peace movement came into existence. As a result nuclear disarmament came into existence. Giddens has called it as Utopian reality.

Globalisation of Modernism: Modernism has given rise to globalisation. The concept of time and place became vast due to modernism. Previously social relations were limited to village, *Panchayat*, block, district, state, pilgrim centres and so on. But now social relation has become global. Time and place has become irrelevant now-a-day. Developed means of communication have made it possible to talk anywhere, to work anywhere, to buy anywhere, and to pay anywhere. All parts of the globe have been integrated. Thus, modernism has been able to integrate the people of the globe.

Post-traditional society: To-day's modern society is also known as post-traditional society. There is no doubt modernity has brought changes in traditional society. But a great part of modern society is still traditional. It has not become free from tradition totally. The post-traditional society has the following characteristics of modernism.

The traditional society has a collective memory. It has continuity. It connects the past with present. The tradition maintains solidarity through collectivity.

- Tradition has religious beliefs and practices. Beliefs and practices are also changing. That is why tradition connects the present with past.
- In tradition there is thoretical truth. That is why people regard their tradition valuable. They regard it as legal. It is very difficult to avoid the procedures of tradition.
- Tradition has morality. It tell us how to behave. It connects us with moral value.

It is really very difficult to break the tradition. But it is possible to add some thing in tradition through modernism. In other words we can say that there is possibility of change in traditon through modernism. In old tradition, people were powerless, but in modern tradition we have power. Now, we have a government of people, for the people and by the people. Today we have been empowered through human rights. Prohibitive actions related to children, women, aged, labours have been taken. A number of traditions have been abolished and a new tradition has been established. Thus, tradition reveals continuity and change both.

FACTORS RESPONSIBLE FOR MAKING MODERNISM AS A DYNAMIC CONCEPT

The following factors keep the modernism as a dynamic concept:

- Ideology of profiteering
- Political Revolutions
- Birth of socialism as a reply to capitalism.
- Victory of liberal ideology
- Contribution of 1989-90 year.
- **Profiteering Ideology:** After the down fall of feudalism, capitalism was established. Capitalism gave rise to profiteering ideology. On account of capitalism and profiteering the world enter into such an economic race whose motive was to get profit more and more. This economic race divided the countries of the globe in two groups—rich countries and poor countries. To get more and more profit new markets were explored. As a result of this colonialism came into existence. British imperialists established industries in Africa and South Asia. Establishment of new and new industries, capitalism and market accelerated the speed of the process of modernisation. This made modernism a dynamic concept.
- **Political Revolutions:** During nineteenth and twentieth centuries a number of political revolution took place. For example French revolution gave rise to a modern charter of citizen right. Due to this revolution, freedom, equality and social Justice became an integral part of common life of man. The state revolution of America also provided the same message to the people. The bloodless state revolution of England was also a new agenda of democratic value. All these revolutions in different countries of the globe provided a form of modernism related to capitalism and democracy. These modern revolutionary values accelerated social, cultural and economic modernism alongwith political

transformation. The capitalism had raised the problem of conflict between traditionality and modernity. This conflict was responsible for modernisation of tradition.

- **Birth of Socialism as Reply to Capitalism:** In Western Europe capitalism provided motion to the modernism. In Eastern Europe an attempt was made to make modernism dynamic through socialism. Socialism came into existence as a reaction against capitalism. But in both systems modernism get its special place. Capitalism and Socialism both are opposable processes, but they have given due importance to modernism in their system.
- **Victory of Liberal Ideology:** The root of liberalism lies in enlightment. It has nourished democracy. It is an enemy of Feudalism and monarchy. Liberalism has played a good role in the establishment of modernism. Modernism has got its expansion due to its liberal ideology. When America faced the situation of defeat in Vietnam war and American economy could not sustain, liberal ideology became strong. Alongwith this event some such books were published in 1980 decade which revealed clearly that modernism could be established through democracy and liberalism.

With liberal authors, Francis Fukuyama, an American scholar wrote his famous book, *The End of History* (1989). In this book Fukuyama related the decrease in power of America to liberalism and modernism. According to him, the history of the globe has met an end. Now, the Western liberal democratic system has been established in the entire world. The evolution of ideology now ended. Now no historical event will take place in the globe. No new ideology will emerge in future. Thus, history of world has ended. Now, the history of world is history of democracy, capitalism, Secularism and modernism. Fukuyama has cited a number of examples in support of his concept the end of history. According to him socialism has been uprooted, religious challenges have got weak, nation-state boundary has become narrowed. These evidences prove that the history of the world can neither move forward nor can go backward. Thus, the end of history has become a phrase of present day history. The political philosophy of liberalism has become phrase of modernism.

- **Contribution of the Year 1989-90**

It is not that modernism has appeared suddenly at global level through strange paths. Rather it has a long history of evolution. The modernism started its journey from the industrial revolution and reached at the end of Feudalism and rise of capitalism. The events which took place in the year 1989-90 provided acceleration to the modernism.

The Europe and America faced major revolutions in the decade 1980-1990. During 1989-90 Poland, Hungary, East Germany, Bulgaria, Czechoslovakia and Romania faced such an astonishing political change which was beyond imagination: The walls of Berlin were felled down. Socialist countries were disintegrated. In the August of 1991 USSR was disintegrated. Now, the world became divided in to democratic capitalism and socialism. The world became unipolar under the system of democratic capitalism. These events proved that modernism based on democratic capitalism is the fate of present day world. But this is not the end of the modernism. A number of scholars are of opinion that modernism coming out of industrial revolution and democratic capitalism has reached to as another storage known as post-modernism.

9
Post-Modernism

Introduction

The school of anthropological thought which sought to question the possibility of impartiality, objectivity or authoritative knowledge is known as school of post-modernism. This school emerged as a general movement during 1980s and 1990s in social science and humanities. The political economists had put the traditional anthropological picture of society and culture at hastened demise. Emergence of post-modernism in social science and humanities has exploded the concept of culture once for all. The theoretical concerns that ethnographers had been to express in 1960s and 1970s were not resolved. Although post-modernism is not a homogenous movement, but post-modernists working within different disciplines, have shared a perspective which emphasises the subjectivity of experience and impossibility of any one form of authoritative knowledge. In anthropology post-modernism has the effect of advancing and refining debate over theoretical and ethical issues raised by political economists. The modernist agenda is not easily dispenses with because it is embodied in key Western assumption about the objective world that can and should be subdued and controlled politically, economically and ideologically—by the orderly, dispassionate and rational Europeans.

In the context of Europe and America post-modernism is not very old concept. It is hardly four and half decade old. Arnold Toyanbee had used the term post-modernism for the first time. At that time he had used this term in the context of Britain. Jean Francois Lyotard had used the concept of post-modernism in his book, *Post Modern Condition* (1979). According to him, post-modernism is a generic concept, not only a creative concept. According to him, modernism had committed two great mistakes which were as follows:

- Concept of Metanarratives
- Myth of Liberalisation

According to Lyotard the theories of metanarratives were now not relevant. The builders of theory of metanarratives were Karl Marx, Emile Durkheim and Max Weber. Their theories of metanarrative was now not acceptable because they had become myths. The first aim of post-modernism was to disapprove the concept of meta-narratives. The second purpose of the post-modernism was to disapprove the myth of liberalisation.

Some Definitions of Post-modernism

There is no unanimity among the scholars regarding definition and meaning of post-modernism. Different scholars have provided different meaning and definition of post-modernism. Some of definitions and meanings of post-modernism are being presented below.

Definition of Gim McGuigan: He was a textbook author. According to him, post-modernism is a cultural and epistemological condition. Modern social institutions are pressed under it and an entry of global society takes place. According to him post-modernism has following characteristics:

- It is a condition of culture and knowledge
- Modern institutions become weak due to it
- It builds a global society

Definition of Richard Gott: According to Gott post-modernism provides us freedom from modernism. It is a fragmental movement. Development of plural culture takes place in it. According to him, post-modernism has following features:

- It makes us free from modern society
- It takes side of fragmentation
- It has cultural plurality

Definition of George Ritzer: Ritzer in his book, *Modernity and Post-Modernity* has attempted to explain the concept of post-modernism. According to him post-modernism is a historical period which begins after the end of modernism. Post-modernism is a cultural concept. It is closely related to art, knowledge, film, archaeology and cultural objects. Post-modern sociological theories are those theories which are different from modern sociological theory. He was of the opinion that post-modernism was a vast concept which included historical period, new cultural elements and new theoreticisation. According to him, post-modernism has following characteristics:

- Post-modernism is a historical period.
- It is related to cultural elements.
- Post-modern theoreticians have disapproved the theory of metanarratives.
- It does not accept foundationalism.

Definition of Jean Francois Lyotard: Lyotard has defined post-modernism as disapproval of metanarratives. For post-modernists metanarratives are not accptable because metanarratives have placed emphasis on whole. But this society is full of diversities. Here one finds social, cultural, economic, political, religious and lingual diversities. In such diverse situation whole cannot be established as theory. He was of the opinion that attention should be paid on local narrtives in place of metanarratives. He had supported fragmentation (locality). He was opponent of totalilty, wholeness and metanarratives. He was related to extraordinary synthesis.

Definition of Jean Baudrillard: Baudrillard has defined post-modernism as hyper reality. Hyper reality is formed by reflex. Mass communication is base of this hyperreality. Symbolic exchanges take place through the medium of mass communication. Therefore drama, stage, pupet dance in modern society. This was the real state of modernism. But later on attempt was made to provide symbol to reality objects through photography, cinema, and T.V. These techniques of communication made real objects symbolic. The objects lost their originality. They became symbols and models. Thus, our world became a copy of reflexive. In this way we can say that post-modenism is hyper reality.

Definition of Fredrick Jameson: Jameson was of the opinion that post-modernism should be viewed from Marxist approach. He has not supported the disapproval of metanarratives. According to him, treating post-modernism as an example of culture is a capitalist system. Beauty has been made sellable commodity of markets in the name of culture. Such cultural organisations as world beauty contest, As is beauty contest, Africa beauty queen contest, Universal beauty contest, Indian beauty contest have made beauty a commodity to be sold in global market. Capitalism in the name of beauty contest is exploiting and oppressing women in the name of culture. Capitalists organise beauty contest. Thus, culture has become slave of capitalists and industrialists.

According to Jameson, post-modernism has following characteristcs:

- Post-modernism has no depth
- It lacks emotions
- It has no history
- It has new technology

Jameson has linked post-modernism with Marxism. He was of the opinion that capitalism was developed in different phases. Today, we are passing through the phase of Late capitalism. Post-modernism has been attached to the cultrual aspects of Late capitalism. Late capitalism has made cutlure sellable. It is selling cultures in the market. Now, cultural things like dance, drama, music, song, art, literature and so on are being sold in markets. The State Government, artists, authors, poets, musician, singers, beauticians, Saints are involved in the business of selling cultures. It has become possible due to late capitalism. The concept of super structure (culture) propounded by Karl Marx cannot be applied in post-modernism. The super structure of post-modernism is pop-culture.

Definition of Michael Foucalt: Foucalt was of the opinion that a great changes has taken place in the post-modern society. This change has influenced our ideas. Today we do not think as we used to think in past. Our way of thinking has changed completely. For example, till middle age, madness was harmless. But now our thinking towards madness has changed. Today madness is a theme of medicine. Now treatment is required in case of madness. We take mad person to a doctor for proper treatment. Foucalt was of the opinion that those who possess discourse, they are powerful in society today. He defined post-modernism as a power embeded in discourse. Logical knowledge is acceptable in every society. Everybody does not possess logical knowledge equally. Logical knowledge has heterogeneity. Today, there is a close relation between power and knowledge. Today only those societies are powerful which have knowledge management.

Definition of Jacques Derrida: According to Derrida, post-modernism can be understood as deconstructionism. This concept has originated from art, literature and films. Its early form was philosophical. But it attained sociological form later on. Attacks have been made on pre-established texts of different areas through deconstructionism. Deconstructionism places emphasis on discovery of meaning expressed in texts. According to him, texts do not reveal social reality. Deconstructionism attempts to explore and analyse the un-expressed meaning of the texts. He was influenced by Ferdenand SauSurre. In the concept of deconstructionism, there is own thinking in understanding the meaning of words. Words are not related to things or extents. Rather they are taken as symbols which has different meanings. The individual has alternative to choose. These words are always deferred.

Definition of Anthony Giddens: According to Anthony Giddnes post-modernism is plural and heterogeneous. Society is not controlled by history or progress. It is not controlled by metanarratives. The post-modernism disapproves the concept of metanarratives and emphasises upon the local narratives. It has put question marks on Jungle of concrete, corporate capitalism and Shining art markets. This has created a new culture termed as Pop culture or popular culture.

Characteristics of Post-modernism

After having a good deal of discussions on definitions and meanings of post-modernism, the following characteristics can be noted:

Post-modernism is a cultural concept: Post-modernism is a cultural concept. This concept is related to social, cultural and political processes. Its expressions can be found in different styles of life. Art, music, song, dance and literatures. This culture can be observed in social function and economic change. Its presence can be felt in positivism, post-structuralism, deconstructionism and frangmentation.

Post-modernism is Multi-dimensional: Modernity used to present unity in diversity. It used to unite diversities. But post-modernism is such a cultural model which represents pluralities. It has fragmentation and locality. It opposes the theory of metanarratives propounded by great social thinkers like Marx, Durkheim and Weber. Post-modernism stresses upon woman, children, aged, tribals, *Dalits*, backwards, blacks and so on.

Post-modernism is against orthodoxy: Most modernism does not support traditions. It supports capitalism on the basis of cultural logic. It is also related to contemporary social, economic and political processes.

Post-modernism supports fragmentation: Post-modernism believes in fragmentation not in whole. It accepts diversities in place of unity. It is not related to continuity. Rather, it deals with discontinuity.

Post-modernism discovers locality: It deals with events on the basis of local or regional area. It observes the relation between social, economic and political processes on the basis of location.

Post-modernism disapproves metanarratives: Post-modernism does not accept the concept of metanarratives. Rather, it believes in local narratives.

Post-modernism supports local autonomy: It nourishes local autonomy. According to it, local people treat modernism as a structure put upon their head. They treat it as a burden which makes themselves. That is why it supports local level movements and conflicts local people believe modernism as an attack from outside.

Post-modernism has no depth: As a theory it does not present an event systemetically. That is why post-modern culture has no depth.

Post-modernism believes in deconstructed personality: Post-modernism is of view that language has no relation with individual. In language word is related to word. As a result deconstructed personality is formed. The deconstructed individuals have deconstructed mentality. Such individuals do not understand their psychological life. They do not understand about their past and future. In other words we can say that post-modernism creates deconstructed individuals who do not have forward or backward vision.

Post-modernism has developed Pop culture: Post-modernism has developed such a culture which is famous as Pop culture. We know about such Pop culture through song, dance, music, art and literature. We can observe such culture in clubs, cinema hall, birthday party, marriage party, music club, entertainment club, and market centres.

Post-modernism has developed consumerism: Post-modernism has made art, dance, music, song, recreation club, literature, cinema hall, restaurant etc. consumerable items. Sale and purchase of culture and cultural items have come into existence. Those who have money travel through aeroplane or A.C. train, A.C. Car, A.C. bus, live in air conditioned house, stay in five or three star hotels, eat delicious and costly restaurant food, buy ticket of costly cinema hall, club, and other recreational centres. They wear costly dresses, and ornaments and have costly furnitures and all modern aemenities in their houses.

Post-modernism has developed sub-culture: It has developed such a culture which is very favourite to youth. It is because this sub culture has made youth free from the bondage of modernism. As a new culture has emerged which is known as sub-culture, this culture is very much in demand among youth of the world.

Post-modernism is a cultural logic: Post-modernism has been accepted as a cultural logic. Special attention is paid on the investment of culture. It has made culture as a thing of investment. This has given rise to cultural capitalism. Now culture is being sold in every parts of the world. Different elements of culture such as art, beauty, music, dance, song, literature and crafts are being sold frequently. Communication media are playing their role in sale and purchase of culture. Folk culture has been named as Pop culture for selling and buying in markets. Females are cutting their hairs and males are increasing their beard. Men are now having no mustache, men and women are wearing same dresses. Cultural corporations and cultural organisations have come into existence. Beauty contests are being organised at world, continent, country, and state level. Sexuality is being aroused though blue films and pronographs. Nakedness has become a thing to be sold and purchased in market. Beauty queens are being marketised, cultural logics are being geven behind all such events. Thus, art, film, and architecture all are cultural logic.

Post-modernism and Anthropology

As discussed earlier in social science and humanity a general movement launched in the decades of 1980s and 1990s is known as post-modernism. Through the ideology of this movement, an attack was made on impartial, objective and authoritative knowledge. According to scholars belonging to this movement, total impartiality or objectivity in the writing of social science and humanities is not possible. The writings of social scientists and scholars of humanities can not be objective and impartial like a natural science. The principle of natural science is same in all times and in all places. But it is not true for social science and humanities. Here, theories get changed according to times and places. It is, therefore, impossible to discover truth and follow scientific method in social science. On this ground, post-modernists have disapproved material, empirical and universal theory. They have not accepted the meta-narratives of Tylor, Morgan, Frazer, Karl Marx, Durkheim, Weber, Spencer, Parsons and Merton. These scholars had attempted to explain society and culture from the point of view of capitalism, industrialism, colonialism and imperealism. They had extended support to political authority and authoritative knowledge. The theories propounded by those great masters were based on authoritative knowledge. These theories were challenged in the light of local and historical contest. The post-modernists suggested local narratives in place of metanarratives. It was because only one theory was not applicable universally so far as art, beauty, music, song, dance, film and literature are concerned. Because they have their own local and historical context. Similarly, no one theory can be applied in anthropology, sociology, fashion, communication and technology. Their theories differ with times and places. Thus, post-modernism makes a deep attack on the root of tradition. It moves forwards on the basis of knowledge and understanding. It does not accept any one grand theory of human behaviour.

Post-modernism places great emphasis upon ideology. It rejects any kind of natural laws. It discredits the concepts of cultural relativism, cross-cultural comparision and universal generalisation. Due to severe attach on previous anthropological theories, post-structuralism, humanism, critical anthropology and cultural study schools have come into existence. The attach by post-modernists came due to two main reasons:

- Failure in making all types of knowledge relative culturally.
- Failure in providing moral support against exploitation and oppression.

Scientific knowledge is not objective. Rather, it is one of methods by which things and events are explained, analysed and described. Anthropology makes study of other cultures. From the point of view of other anthropology has been ethnic centred. Due to failure of cultural relativism anthropologists had to face severe criticism. Great anthropological masters never extended moral support to exploited, oppressed and deprived groups.

Some anthropological facts related to post-modernism are as follows:

- Attempt to discover truth related to human behaviour was never made through social studies. Whatever truth we know, they are determined by culture. It has no relation with objective truth.
- Human sacrifice and canabolism are not wrong from the point of view of value of communities practicing them. Such events must be explored, explained and analysed from their point of view. They may be manifestations of their culture about which we know nothing. A researcher can not judge such practices from his own value.
- Biologists study the organisms with the help of microscope which causes diseases and prescribe medicine for remedy. The priest and magician see the spirits who cause diseases and harms. They, have their, own techniques and provide fetishes and *Jharphuk* for remedy of diseases. In this situation we cannot say that doctor is right and the priest magician is wrong.

Post-modernism has brought a number of problems before us to solve in anthropology. They are as follows:

- Anthropolgoy is not a science.

- Anthropology is an interpretive science in which explanation of meaning is done. Anthropology is harmeneutics basically.
- This is quite wrong that European male maintains objective bases in study of other cultures by isolating himself from his own cultures.
- Ethnographies are half-partial and subjective.
- All theories are political naturally. Their value judgement should be made by knowing their impact on people.
- Ethnographies are basically texts. In changed situations, new ethnographic style should be developed.

It is true that social-cultural study cannot be objective completely. The subjective idea of observer does not remain completely detached. The subjectivity of observer influences the obseved phenomena. Therefore, he does not remain impartial and bias free. He becomes partial and biased. That is why the real meaning of seen phenomena remains confusing. Therefore, anthropological study cannot be scientific.

In the eyes of post-modernists, all theories and concepts propounded by great anthropological thinkers, Tylor, Morgon, Maine, Mclennan, Bachofen, Bastian, Frazer, Boas, Malinowski, Radcliffe-Brown, Margaret Mead and so on were far away from objectivity. They were not scientific. They never explained cause effect relationship. The work of an anthropologist should not be to explain cultural events. Rather his aim should be to know the meaning hidden behind the cultural events.

Through the medium of post-modernism, weakness of anthropological ethnographies were brought to light. Post-modernists were of the view that majority of ethnographies were written by those scholars who claimed themselves as pan observer. It was not possible for any one observer. He could not understand the whole complexity of a culture. He could not provide an objective description of culture isolating his own subjectivity. Thus, those ethnographies were not objective, impartial and bias free. Anthropologists had also used ornamental terms in their ethnographies. They had written their ethnographies by collecting informations from few informants. Those field works also had limitation of time and place. Inspite of these weaknesses, they claim their ethnographies objective and impartial.

But infact they gathered insufficient informations from few informants and generalised their findings. In ethnography we do not find the name of Informants involved in hunting. Rather we find the name of tribe involved in hunting. These ethnographies do not mention the situation in which hunting was done and the fieldwork was carried out. We do not find mention of period of fieldwork. The generalisations of White Europeans and Americans were taken as truth, authoritatve and objective.

Post-modernists want to make a drastic change in the themes and research methodology of Anthropology. They are in favour of multi-dimensional research so that they can face the challenges occuring at global level successfully. Unlike post-ethnography, readers of present day ethnographies are also members of those communities about whom ethnography has been written. According to post-modernists, the end of colonialism, major demogratphic change, large scale migration in Europe and America from Asia and Africa, knowledge and information revolution, nuclear bomb destruction and digital revolution have created such a situation in which our traditional knowledge is loosing its roots. Such events have influenced the people of entire globe. Anthropology is facing a great challenge due to such global level events. Such global level events cannot be studied by old or traditional anthropological methods. They cannot be explained in old ethnographic style. The post-modernists have introduced new approaches, methods, techniques, styles and themes for anthropological research.

Post-modernists have also been subjected to criticism. Crtics do not agree with post-modernists that anthropology is not a science. For them anthropology is an impirical science. According to them under the shadow of subjectivity anthropology is objective science. If we take post-modernists criticism as true, then anthropology will become only a branch of literature. But this is not acceptable.

Contributions of Post-modern Thinkers and their Theory

It is fitness of the thing to present here the contribution of post-modern thinkers one by one. Here we are going to deal with the contributions of following post-modern thinkers.

- Paul Feyerband
- Michel Foucault
- Bourdieu
- Jean Baudrillard
- Jean Francois Lyotard
- Jacques Derrida
- Fredric Jameson
- Anthony Giddens
- Marcus
- Fischer

Post-modernism of Paul Feyerband

In social science and humanities, Post-modernism was initiated as a movement in 1980s and 1990s decades. This movement had brought a challenge on traditional ethnographies and objective, impartial and authoritative knowledge of anthropology. Even after arrival of post-modernism in anthropology, it was not easy to dispense the modernist agenda. It was because modern agenda was embeded in Western assumption about the objective world that can and should be subdued and controlled-politically, economically and ideologically by orderly dispassionate and rational Europeans.

An early critic of modernism was philosophical anarchist Paul Feryband. He argued that there was no logical way to choose between conventional scholarly models or paradigms. The concept of paradigm had come from the historian and philosopher of science Thomas Kuhn. In his highly influential book, *The Structures of Scientific Revolutions* (1962), he argued that science is not commulative. It does not necessarily progress towards clearer understanding and truth. According to him, science is conventional. It consists of answers to questions raised by scientists at a particular time and particular place. According to Kuhn, this period of normal science yields results for a while. But, non-conforming observations eventually instigate scientific revolution. Now old questions are superseded by new questions to which observations conform. A new period of normal science ensues, until other non-conforming observations instigate another scientific revolution. Kuhn has called the intellectual framework for normal science a "Paradigm". He has termed the process of scientific revolution, "a Paradigm shift". He cited the example of paradigm shift from Aristotelian to Newtonion science in scientific revolution of seventeenth century. His main point to highlight was that new paradigm are not necessarily superior to old ones. Paradigms are only different and incommensurable.

Feyerband argued that there is no logical way to choose between paradigms because all such explanations are inevitably explanations. According to him scientific thought and institutions are the product of lived experience as are their assumption about truth or authoritative knowledge. The truth claimed by scientists cannot be understood as superior to other manner of explanation for social phenomena. Rather all explanations are basically incommensurable. An important insight of anthropologists in recent years has been that modernity has carried forward these ideals since sixteenth century. The modernist perspective itself constitutes an invented tradition. The product of creative social action through time, not a revealation or awakening to true understanding of an external objective realilty. This revolution in perspective has caused great excitement and upheaval in humanities and social science. A number of scholars have come forward to make significant contribution in developing a post-modern perspectives, but two French scholars, Foucalt and Pierre Bourdieu have influenced the course of anthropological theory.

Post-modernism of Michael Foucault

Michael Foucault was born at Poyafers in France on 15th October, 1926. He died in Perisu on 25th June, 1984. Foucault was greatly influenced by Karl Marx. Being influenced by Marx, he has criticised all existing theories. Marx had opined that labour class would establish socialism in the world through their revolution. But Foucault had not established any such forecast. But theories propounded by him brought a revolution in the thinking of his contemporary.

Major contributions of Foucault are as follows:

- Madness and civilisation 1961
- The Birth of the clinic 1963
- Discipline and Punish 1975
- History of sexuality 1975

Foucault was full of qualities. He was philosopher, scholar, expert of culture and society, historians and politician. When he had joined as Professor in Vincenage University as a Professor in Philosophy, his complete politcalisation had taken place. He was actively engaged in politics within campus and outside campus when violation of human rights had started. Foucault had gone to Iran to lead the movement against Shah. When new socialist party came to power in France, inhabitants of Polands had become victims of oppression and deprivation. He had oppossed the socialist oppression. He had gone to Poland to establish a compromise between intellectuals and labour organisations. Besides Marx, he was also influenced by Weber, Levi-Strauss and Ferdenand Sausurre.

The post-modernism of Foucault can be understood in the following ways:

- Crime, madness and sexuality should be understood in the context of jail and hospital.
- In the state of evolution Enlightment and Renaissance were supporter of freedom of individuals. But they were also interested in controlling man. Thus, the reciprocal relationship between power, ideology and discourse should be seen in the context of modern organisational system.
- According to Foucault, discourse is a concept of common people. It is their thinking. It is a common view of people regarding a thing. What people think about criminal, madness and sexuality, what they have opinion towards them, is known as discourse.
- Power works through the medium of discourse. The power has no meaning in itself. To make power meaningful, discourse is a must. The concept of people regarding a thing can be changed. It is the work of power to make a change in the concept of the people. With the help of power a change is brought in traditional discourse or thinking.
- Foucault had opposed the common acceptance related to the nature of science. He had a doubtful approach towards the nature of science. The approach of Foucault was different from general social scientists. General social scientists make a comparison of known thing with unknown things. But

comparing the known things with unknown things, general social scientists attempt to know about the unknown things. Contrary to this approach, Foucault, has attempted to discover unknown things of past and gather knowledge about them. In this way Foucault explains known things after discovering the past unknown things.

- Foucault has heavily criticised the modern visible ideas, faiths, traditions, concepts and structures. He has criticised them because they were known. After criticising them, he turned towards crime, madness and sexuality which were unknown since past. Thus, he discovered first unknown things to explain the known things.
- Modern society has changed into post-modern society due to change in discourse or understanding.
- Discourse of power is present in different types of roles in society.

CONTRIBUTION IN ARCHAEOLOGY OF KNOWLEDGE

The centre point of Foucault Post-modernism is the concept of discourse. We have scientific and logical discourse of the individuals and things of the society in which we live today. The archaeology of knowledge was the earlier work of Foucault. The English translation of the book had appeared in 1989. Like other post-modernists, Foucault was also interested in epistemology. He wanted to know the nature of science, what are its source and what is its origin. If we get information about the knowledge, we can make human life efficient beautiful and happy. The chief interest of Foucault was not in materials available from archaeological sites or material cultural traits discovered from the archaeological sites. He was interested in those techniques and theories of archaeology which influenced, regularised and controlled the thinking of people. To discover the discourse hidden behind material cultural traits available from archaeological sites was the main aim of Foucault. He wanted to know the discourse of prehistoric man. He observed that in the construction of discourse among prehistoric man subjects were secondary. Subjective thinking about the objects was irrelevent. The importance of subject emerged in nineteenth century. Humanism emerged in modernism. Now, the importance of subject or individual was increased. Thus, the origin of discourse or knowledge of prehistoric and ancient historic things and events were in people not in subject.

In course of study of archaeology, Foucault came to know that the interest of prehistoric people was in object not in subject. But in modern period the interest of people was changed from object to subject. In archaeological period people were objective, but they become subjective in modern period. During modern period people recognised the importance of subject. They began to think what subject was? What is its reality. The turn in history and culture is product of subject. The history is witness that a subject makes another subject bounded. Foucault has discussed the expression of subjects in different forms such as master, servants, labour, artisan, workers, individual, oppressed, exploited, deprived, humiliated, safe and unsafe.

In the archaeology of knowledge he arrived at such a conclusion that defined man as such knowledge which could bring a new turn in the history. It is knowledge which makes an individual powerful, knowledge makes a man master, capitalist, industrialist, labour, worker, servant, slave and unsafe. In archaeology the knowledge was a triangle of power, knowledge and individual. Knowledge has not been same in all periods. Knowledge has changed according to time. Knowledge has defined subject in different periods.

CONTRIBUTION ON MADNESS AND CIVILISATION

In his book, *Madness and Civilisation* (1961), Foucault brought the problem of cause and uncause into light. The English version of this book was published in 1989. Foucault began with his obsevation on madeness in different historical period. He found that mads were kept in society previously. They were not isolated from the society. But for the first time in Europe mads were isolated from the society and kept in a separate house known as *Pagalkhana* (Home of Mad). Before this, theft, docoits, criminals and beggars were kept in jail. In 1974, a French doctor had released all mads or abnormals from the Philipe Pinele Besentre hospital to keep them in separate remanud home or *Pagalkhana* (Home of abnormals or mads). To Foucault, this event was not a subject of humanism and enlightment. Rather it was an act of hollow idealism. Because all freed abnormals were kept in an another home meant for them. Thus, it was not a symbol of humanism or idealism. It was a discourse of power.

Foucault had made a study of mads and abnormals from medieval to enlightment period. Clinical Psychology was born in the period of enlightment. During medieval period, clinical psychology had not emerged. With the emergence of clinical psychology clinics were established for the treatment of madness and abnormalities in scientific way. Now, madness and abnormalities were treated with the help of mediciene after clinical analysis. For Foucault it was a historical period of cause and effect. In this way episticmology was the centre of this book.

According to Foucault madness and cause were not isolated during renaissance. One was cause and the other was effect. There was a reason behind being mad or abnormal. There was no silence between madness and cause. There was a conversation between madness and cause. It was generally total that he/she became mad or abnormal due to his/her poor economic condition, family ward, death of beloved ones, dacoity, theft and so on. In this way a conversation was established between cause and effect of madness. This conversation between cause and effect of madness was maintained in renaissance. But this conversation was broken during medieval period (1680-1800). There was a silence between cause and effect of madness. When clinical science emerged as a power, it began to explain madness in its own way. Now, the knolwedge became power. Knowledgeable persons became powerful. An administration was established between knowledge and power or discourse of power was established. In France lacs of people were kept in Jails, remand house; rehabilitation homes and so on in the name of mad as abnormal, unemployed and beggars. It is because knowledgeable elite class people do not want to stay with them. They cannot adjust with them. On the basis of their earned power of knowledge, the powerful elites make them prisoners and force them to stay away from the society. These works are performed by those who are experts, who have knowledge and who have power. In fact they have discourse of power. The explanation of madness is done by doctors and explanation of crime is done by Judge. In this way mads and criminals are sent in remand home, rehabilitation home or Jail through the learned persons or experts who possess sufficient knowledge in those fields. In this way a discourse of power has been established among knowledge, power and individual as we have entered in the civilisation.

CONTRIBUTION ON THE BIRTH OF CLINIC: AN ARCHAEOLOGY OF MEDICAL PERCEPTIONS

The English version of this book was published in 1973. This book has given a new thought related to medicine. According to Foucault there has been change in medical system. In entire eighteenth century, medicine was a classificatory science. Diseases were identified by touching pulses. In nineteenth century examination of dead body began. The examination of dead body gave rise to the knowledge of internal structure of human body. Disease related study of dead bodies gave us special knowledge about diseases of heart, chest, liver, kidney, gall bladder, intestine and so on. As a result of such observations and examination of different internal parts of dead human bodies, specialist doctors came into existence. Now medical science was not a classificatory science, but it became disease-oriented science. The importance of clinical observation increased. The knowledge of medical science explains that doctors have become powerful due to their special knowledge. They have come between life and death. Discourse of knowledge, management of knowledge has made doctors a great powerful. In this way, knowledge, power and subject are related reciprocally.

CONTRIBUTION ON DISCIPLINE AND PUNISH

Discipline and Punish: The Birth of Prison was published in 1979 in English Verson. This book is an important contribution on the crime and prison system. During medieval period in England criminals were punished physically. The physical punishment was eye for eye, teeth for teeth, hand for hand, head for head and leg for leg. But when prison came into existence, a revolutionary change in way of punishment to criminal took place. Now, a system of controlling the mind of criminals in place of physical punishment was developed. Now-a-day criminals are not punished physically. Rather they are kept in Jail or imprisonment. They are isolated from the rest of society.

The system of physical punishment during medieval period reveals that authority were powerful. They had power on the basis of which they punish criminals physically. Capitalists had authority over power. Jail system or prison system is a capitalist system. Prison system is closely related to disciplinary power. It was a pre-condition for capitalism. Through this system disciplinary power is excercised in various social areas such as hospital, school, Army and industries, Through this system the capitalist interests are protected.

CONTRIBUTION ON SEXUALITY: SPEAKING OF SEX

Foucault wanted to produce his thesis on Sexuality in six volumes, but he could produce only three volumes which are as follows:

- History of Sexuality (1978, 1980) Volume-I
- The Use of Pleasure (1984, 1985) Volume-II
- The Care of the Self (1984, 1986) Volume-III

In his Ist and IInd volumes, Foucault has laid emphasis on Sexuality of Western Society. In his third Volume Foucault has explained the Sexuality of Greece and Rome before Christ. In all his three Volumes, Foucault has dealt with knowledge, power and individual. According to him, there is a close relation between knowledge, power and sexuality. He has observed that public discussion on sexuality in the beginning of seventeenth century was prohibited in European Society. Its discussion was limited to family and marital life. On the basis of religion and morality public discussion on sexuality was prohibited. It was also prohibited to take the names of those organs dealing with sex at public places. But in eighteenth century, sexuality was eroded and enhanced. The owner or authorities of power criticised the pleasure of sex. They used sex as means of entertainment, pleasure and enjoyment. The sexuality became ths slave of king, Raja, Maharaja, emperor and capitalists. Sex became a commodity to be sold or purchased for pleasure and satisfaction of passion. Now, an open discussion was started on sex. Thus, a triangle was established between knowledge, power and sex (individual).

During eighteenth century, the problem of population growth appeared in Europe. Now, Sexuality became a social and economic problem. Now, sexuality was correlated to population growth. Demography came into existence to study the socio-economic characteristics of population. Now, sexuality became a serious problem. Sex life and sex behaviour became a subject to be discussed at public places. What should be the marriage age, at what age marriage should take place, how selection of marriage mates be done. How many children a couple should reproduce, what should be the gap between birth of two children, what methods should be employed to prevent unwanted birth or to maintain a gap between two births, what is safe sex relation, how safe sex relation can be maintained, what is AIDS, how it spreads, how it can be prevented and so on are discussed frequently not only in family and marital life, but also at public places by different Governmental and Non-Governmental agencies. In this way now-a-day, sexuality is viewed as a problem. This vision has changed the contact of sexuality. According to Foucault, sexuality may be a symbol of love and morality for some one. For some one else it may be an art of love, feeling of beauty, expression of art and identification of love.

Sexuality is also expressed in such terms which reveal only sexuality. In Christian religion sex morality loosers have to seek repentance. In post-modern society sex is a matter of the Government. The Government runs a number of programmes for controlling sexuality. Sex education is being imparted. Previously sex problems were solved by the advice of Priest, elders and doctors. Now, we have a full flaged medical system for this purpose. There are family doctors and Governmental and Non-Governmental Organizations who extend their help in solving the problems of sexuality. The control of sexuality now is in the hand of experts. Experts possess knowledge of sexuality. That is why they have become powerful as experts. In this way knowledge, power and sexuality (individual) have become integrated. They have formed a golden triangle to control sexuality.

FOUCAULT'S CONCEPT OF POWER

According to Foucault power is not an efficiency or ability of anybody. It is not an achievement which can be exchanged. It is not a synonym of any structure or institution. It has neither a form, nor a place. It is not primarily negative and destructive. According to Foucault power is related to such a force which is present in all social structures. It is present in all social relations. All social relations are infact power relation. The power has no existence in isolation. It is always found in social relation. Power is impartial in its influence. It operates like force. Power is definitely related to institutions. For example family, school, college, university, prison, hospital, remand home, aged home, nursing home, factory, army, club and so on. There is reciprocal relation between knowledge and power. Power cannot be isolated from the knowledge. According to Foucault, such a process between knowledge, power and man goes which enriches both knowledge and individual. Knowledge enriches individuals and individual enriches knowledge. Individual gets benefit from knowledge and he enriches the storage of knowledge. Thus, a triangle is formed between knowledge, power and individual.

Foucault has expressed body as power. When he has talked about knowledge, power and individual, he has talked about body in place of individual. An individual has biological power. Body in takes power and reproduces power. But now-a-days, biological power has been put under the control of disciplinary power. The organic power of individual becomes secondary before disciplinary power. Individual has become powerless. By disciplinary power such a body is created which may always remain under the control of discipline and management. A body is prepared for it. For example, life, drill, prayer, class, work stratification, place, control etc.

Michael Foucault was a historian of culture. He viewed social institutions and relationships being ultimately grounded in a pervassive economy of discourses of power. Discourses of power shape relations between people at all levels in society. Discourses of power is a phrase coined by Foucault to describe the heterogeneous spectrum of institutions, rhetoric's, tactics and strategies employed by one group to dominate another group ideologically, politically and economically. The many different roles played by individuals—employers, employees, doctors, patients, priest, faithful, teacher, students—all bear certain kinds of relations between people in which some dominate and others are subjugated. Whoever dominate these relations also controls the economic and ideological conditions under which knowledge or truth are defined. Dominating classes inscribe their power through a series of tactics and strategies that instruct people behaviour a certain way in the world. In this way, beginning with enlightment and rise of nation-state in eighteenth century discourses of sentimental/sexualtiy and humanism became dominant in European society, preserving their power through mechanism of control such as prisons, hospitals, asylums, and museums. Foucault was interested as to how power determines different social forms through history. Because modernity is viewed as configuration of knowledge, as the product of power, the objective character of socialistic knowledge is shown to be a historical construct.

POST-MODERNISM OF PIERRE BOURDIEU

Like Foucault, Pierre Bourdieu has also addressed similar issues relating to power and domination. But he has approached the problem from an another angle. Bourdieu's theory places the social actor at the centre of social process. Unlike Foucault whose theory views individuals and their relationship as being determined by discourses of power, Bourdieu holds that these arrangements are created by human agents. Human agents assemble their cultures through practice or Praxis. The concept of practice or Praxis was pioneered by Bourdieu holding that society and culture are constructed by purposeful creative agents who bring life to their society and culture through talk and action, making their creations appear to be objective facts of nature rather than arbitrary constructs imagined and assembled by the people. What people do in practice is to create, reproduce and change a variety of taxonomies that are understood to be basis of social relations. These taxonomies are made up of symbolic representations that do not merely reflect ideas about the world, but make the world what it is for the people who are in it. The individuals are powerful to the extent that they can impose on others taxonomies that reproduce their own power and authority. The individuals are powerless to the extent that they are unable to escape from their social positioning in relation to taxonomies created by others. Either way, the taxonomies wielded by the powerful in relation to powerless are only relevent in so far as they are lodged within a configuration of social relations.

In the thought of Bourdieu the notion of relational is so significant because it helps to move social sciences from those various formulations of social strucutre as conceived by earlier generation Durkheimean thinkers. Bourdieu was of the view that structures and cultures are not to be compared with a machine or organism. It is because culture and society are ultimately not things, rather they are system of relationships or fields. Bourdieu has fourmulated the concept of fields to describe every dynamic configuartion or network of objective relationships between social agents and positions. Thus, he has defined field as fluid open ended networks of objective relations between positions. Complex societies are comprised of any number of fields such as artistic, intellectual, economic, religious, political, educational, health and so on. Although co-existing temporarily and spatially these fields are nevertheless descrete and integrated according to their own internal logic. Within fields, the total impositioning one group's set of taxonomies upon another's results in the production of a natural order or doxa. The concept of doxa was used by Bourdieu to describe a state in which all members of a community take for granted the naturalness of relation within the community, regardless of social, economic and political inequalties. In doxa the essentially arbitrary character of powerful taxonomies is obscured. For powerful and powerless both what emerges alike in sense that certain feelings, thought and actions are part of outer objective world, while others (those of dominated) are unnatural.

In short, the social relations are actually the result of one interest group's symbolic domination over the other group within a society. What is seen to be real is invariably reflects of point of view of whoevers interests are served by that reality. Unlike Foucault's model in which individuals are dominated by a powerful system, Bourdieu believes that individual actors are able to create alternative taxonomies that resist those that powerful seek to impose. The well spring of this individual agency is the habitus or the ways in which personal history and social positioning allow individuals to improvise or rennovate. The concept of habitus was formulated by Bourdieu to describe the capacity of individuals to rennovate social and cultural form based on their personal history and social positioning within a community.

In the decades of 1980 and 1990 Foucaults and Bourdieu's ideas have had a dramatic impact on anthropological theory. Depending on one's sympathies, their work has been highly illuminating or deeply mystifying. For many researchers there seemed to be no firm ground from which students of human life could gaze objectively at their subject matter. Henceforth, no truth would be taken for granted and no perspectives left unchallenge.

Now, deconstruction became a new watch word for anthropologists. The term deconstruction was used as an ambition of post-modernism to understand the political and cultural context hidden behind the writing or construction of philosophical, literary, historical and ethnographic narratives. Some have mistaken post-modernists stand as against the existence of objective reality. They have accused post-modernist researches of Solipsism. Solipsism is an idea that individual self is the only reality and that the whole external world exists only in one's imagination or dream state. Bourdieu has discussed his theory in detail in his book, *Outline of a Theory of Practice*.

POST-MODERNISM OF GEORGE MARCUS

In anthropology post-modern perspective has been most influential in the writing of ethnography. Anthropologists working in 1980s and 1990s were extremely conscious of the subjective nature of the documents they had produced. James Clifford and George Marcus edited Volume, *Writing Culture: the Poetics and Politics of Ethnography* (1986) was influencial particulary in advancing the ideas that cultural accounts are constructed texts and that the relation between writer, reader and text or subject matter of ethnography are complex and problematic. Whereas standard interpretive approaches have viewed subjects as creative actors, constructing their social words out of symbols, post-modernists have noted with deep irony that these same ethnographers previlege their own status as external observers. In other words it can be said that while every body was forced to build culture, anthropologists were exempted from this process. It was for them to observe rather than to be observed. In contrast, post-modernists argue that ethnographies, no less than any other form of creative writing, are texts that previlege the perspective of their author. This insight has had deep implications for anthropological theory. Because the account which we get is a result of a special type of approach. It is related to writer and his interest. Real objectivity is impossible. Even if a researcher makes study of a non-formal object, he or she does not find time to use analytical classification. The division of ethnographic project into subject and object reveals the impact of modernism on anthropological thought.

POST-MODERNISM OF FISCHER

Fischer was an American Post-modernist. He was a close associate of Marcus. He in his edited book with Marcus, *Anthropology A Cultural Critic: An Experimental Movement in Human Sciences* (1968) has propounded his theory of post-modernism. According to him, anthropology has began to work as cultural critic in the period of post-modernism. In the period of post-modernism a number of experimental movements have been started in anthropology. As a result anthropology has started functioning as cultural critic. He has dealt with impact of information technology, computer, cinema, T.V. under his post-modernism.

Recognising the real objectivity, new generation anthropologists have attempted to remove the ethical and methodological confusion created by post-modern theories. New generation anthropologists have devised such a way by which description of different cultures and societies could be presented without rejecting the subjectivity of people and description of realistic knowledge. Being influenced by Foucault and Bourdieu, new generation anthropologists developed such strategy which shows that the subject of ethnography creates categories of meaning which is helpful in collecting informations related to their collective world. This methodology is known as social constructionism. The concept of social constructionism was propounded by Peter Burger and Thomas Luckman. Through this methodology an attempt was made to show as to how ethnographic subject uses language and provides a pattern of activities. Through this how he creates cultural meaning, how he maintains continuity and how he brings changes. Thus, ethnographic subject has influened greatly to anthropological writing now-a-day. Now-a-day attempt has been made to bring out definite nature of cultural meaning.

Benedict and Anderson in their book, *Imagined Community* (1883) has reconstructed the concept of nation-state. According to them, a nation is all imagined set of a special social and historical condition.

Errik Hubsbam and Terence Rauger in their edited book, *The Intention of Tradition* (1992) have presented a collection of historical essays. In these essays attempts have been made to discuss the invented origin of modern traditions and characters. They were recognised as ancient markers of ethnological identity.

POST-MODERNISM OF JEAN BAUDRILLARD

Jean Baudrillard was a French theoretician who was mainly interested in means of communication. In the formulation of post-modern theory his achievements are as follows:

- Mass communication media are playing significant role in post-modern society. In fact post-modern society is mass media society.
- Post-modern society in reality is consumption society.
- Post-modern society is image society or simulation society.
- Some theories may be propounded in relation to post-modernism.

In the beginning of his life he was deeply influenced by Karl Marx. Marx used to discuss production relation throughout his life. The base of his theory was production relation. Being influenced by his production relation, Baundrillard presented a change in the theory of Marx. Marx had never discussed about the consumption. Baundrillard made the consumption a central point of his theory. Along with consumption, he made a special emphasis on economic and material processes of culture. He made explanation of culture on the basis of economic and material processes. He was also influenced by structuralist Ferdenand Saussure. Being influenced by Saussure he had propounded the view that nature of language is not individual, rather the nature of language is social. In the structure of language symbols and images plays significant role. He propounded the symbolic exchange theory.

Baudrillard was also influenced by Durkheim. Durkheim has brought to the light the tradition of gift exchange. According to Durkheim, primitives used to do reciprocal exchange of women as gift in the kinship system. Besides, on the occasion of birth, marriage, death, festivals they used to do reciprocal exchange of gift in the form of commodities among friends and relatives. This was an economic material process. Baudrillard propounded the theory of symbolic exchange in place of Durkheim's Socio-economic exchange theory. According to Baudrillard, in simple or folk societies exchange of symbols not exchange of objects takes place on the occasion of birth, marriage, death, worship and festivals among friends and relatives. According to him, worship, sacrifice, feast, *prasad, Haria* (rice beer) wine, etc. are symbols not objects which are exchanged on different social and religious occasions. Symbolic system keeps members of simple or folk societies united and makes their world cognizible. On the bases of mass media, consumption, image, symbols, symbolic system and symbolic exchange, Baudrillard has attempted to propound his theory of post-modernism.

Important Contribution of Baudrillard

His important contributions in the form of books are as follows:

- The selected writing (edited) 1988.
- The mirror of production, 1975.
- Simulation 1973
- The Masses
- The estacy of communication 1985.
- Symbolic exchange and death 1976
- The system of objects 1968.

All post-modernists have made a discussion on epistemology essentially. Post-modernists had also attempted to understand the reality of knowledge. They had made attempt to understand the reality of society. They had taken logic and experience into consideration to find out reality.

They were of the opinion that on the basis of rationalism and empericism, attempt can be made to distinguish the truth from untruth. Baudrillard has attempted to analyse the reality of contemporary society. According to Baudrillard, production method and production relation have now no dominance on contemporary society. Now-a-day, contemporary society has impact of cybernetic model, steering system, computer, internet, communication media, information technology, entertainment and knowledge related industries. In modern society profiteering and exploitation were prevalent. But in post-modern society symbolism is prevalent. In post-modern society symbols and reality have been inter-linked so deeply that it is difficult to isolate them today. Our society is what T.V. presents before us. Through the medium of different symbols presented by T.V. we are attracted towards beautifying creams, energetic medicine, tooth paste, clothes, edible oils, soap, surf, refine oil, medicine of sex related disease. Small family, gap between two children and so on. Behaviour of post-modern society is now based on symbols. Electronic and print media have made the symbolic system more and more strong. We are, now, only image of T.V. and Print media. Production society has changed into consumption society. Now, the basis of stratification in society is not production, rather, it thas become consumption. Now, he is placed at upper stratum who has more and more consumption efficiency. Now, the basis of discrimination in society is consumption. Consumption is determined by media and symbols.

According to Baudrillard Post-modern society is a dasaling or glittering society. It is far away from reality. It is known as Diznyland. Diznyland is a name of park in America. This park has a cartoon films of children. This cartoon film is full of confusion and reality. Like Diznyland, the post-modern society recognises symbols, images and carbon copy as real. This is known as simulation.

According to Baudrillard Simulation is different categories which the modernity, which came in the first stage of simulation, was termed as early modernity. This early modernity period was from renaissance to French revolution. In the stage of renaissance, the society was Feudal society. It was based on inequality. In this age classes were closed. There was no mobility.

Early modernity was broken by industrial revolution. This was a second category of simulation. Later on technological revolution took place. Now large scale production became the phrase of the society. After Second World War third category of simulation appeared. It gave birth to post-modernism.

Marx had discussed modern society only in the context of political economy. He had paid attention on capital, but not on non-economic aspects of production. Advertisement, media, information technology and net work also influence the production.

Baudrillard has established the theory of post-modernism by moving away from Marx. Previously attention was made on utility value of production. But now-a-day attention is paid on models, symbols, symbolic system, symbolism and simulation. Attempt has been made to create hyper reality by media. Today's society is full of hypocrisy, hypomania, vulgarity. We are copying these things which are not real. They are far away from reality. Now, there is no difference between real object and carbon copy. When copy becomes inseperable part of life, then it can not be isolated from the reality. On this ground Baudrillard is known as Nihilist theoretician. The facts related to post-modernism of Baudrillard area as follows:

- Media and public
- Image or simulation
- Hyper reality
- Consumption society
- Symbol
- Symbolic exchange
- Fashion
- Hypermania.

Media and Public

According to Baudrillard the society in whicih we live is a copy of Western society. It is known as simulation or image society. In this society there is no difference between mirror and photo. Mirror is photo. Whatever mirror tells is taken as true, real and correct. News media create hypermania. Previously, there was a difference between individual life and public life. There was a taboo to enter in the bedroom of a couple. Now, television has made individual life a common life. Now, couple, children, friends, and relative sit together in the same bedroom where couple spends night. T.V. and films have brought those relatives closer who were incests culturally. Members belonging to different age and sex group sit together and enjoy vulgar picture or scenes or T.V. or films. In T.V. and films we are far away from reality. We do not have any experience of reality. We see only those things which T.V. films present before us. We accept them as real and truth. Now, T.V. is our world. On T.V. screen we see semi-naked or naked women in inner or thiner. We see men having long hairs with ornaments in neck, ears, nose, hands and fingers, we see scene of love affairs, unsuitable marriage, same sex marriage, live in relationship, intercaste and inter-religion marriage, surrogacy and so on. Demands of ponography and blue films have increased. We enjoy sexuality, vulgarity, hyperreality, hypocrisy and hypomania. The media has made our individual life a public life.

Mass media has defined time and space in new perspectives. We are bound to live in such a world where there is more and more informations and less and less meaning. Print and electronic media has presented before us a huge storage of informations. Baudrillard has used the term simulation to know the relation between media and public.

Simulation

According to Baudrillard, there is lack of origional copy in this age of post-modernism. In this age of information technolgoy there is no original copy. All are images or copies. News transmitted on T.V. and advertisement are frangmented image. We find here hyper reality. All informations are taken from the history. But history of new is rejected.

Image or carbon or photocopies are copies of those copies which do not have original copy. They have no relation with reality. Advertising companies do not show the real price of things so that they could earn profit more and more. Talking Diznyland of Los Angeles, Baudrillard opines that it presents an interesting story of American society in very beautiful manner. It highlights American values and ideals. But it does not reveal the reality of American society. It does not reveal the ugly images of American which have made poor nation more poor, which threatens the entire countries of the world through wars, which has established its army stations everywhere in the name disarmament and democratic system, which believes in war for selling its arms and so on. Thus, simulation presents a picture of image society which is not real. Some examples of simulations are as follows:

- South American tribes are now leading their life in simulation.
- Through simulation nuclear war between Russia and America was sown during *Khari Yudha* (Gulf War).
- In Iraq war propaganda of biological weapon disarmament was made through simulation.
- Through simulation, attack on Afghanistan was justified as a step towards curbing terorism.

Thus, a cover is placed on reality through simulation.

Hyper Reality

According to Baudrillard, simulation has acquired such a universality and popularity to-day in post-modern World that there is no reality anywhere. If we have something, that is hyper reality. Reality about which media tells us is that reality which cannot be criticised logically. Baudrillard has made a distinction between information and communication. Communication is a two way process, whereas information is one way process. T.V. presents a real thing as hyper real. This has removed the confusion between real and ideal. Everything in today's post-modern world is hyper. Hyper reality is created by T.V. programme. In this situation, the reality which we accept today is not reality, rather it is a reality created by T.V. that is why it is hyper reality.

According Baudrillard, Simulation has passed through different stages. Its first phase was between renaissae and industrial revolution. Its second phase appeared in industrial period. In this period automatic machines and refrigerator were invented. In the third phase of post-modern period, mods were built in place of industrial production. These models were not of production, rather they were of reproduction. Through these models fashion, media, advertisement, information, communication and network made their appearance in the society. Today's capitalism is known as late capitalism which is based on simulation. The culture of today has reached in such a stage where there is no solution. Now, there is no spiritual power to save the cancer infected today's society. This is fourth stage of simulation. This is known as fractured order.

Consumption Society

Baudrillard has talked about, his post-modernism through mass media. He has talked about simultation, hyper reality and symbols. Present day society is consumption society and information society. Media has made this society consumer. It is media which creates demand. In this way Baudrillard has used consumption as an explanatory tool in place of production. In production society utility value is important. But in post-modern consumption society sign value or symbol value is important. The high sign value object has high price. It is sign value which determines the price value of things. There has been increase in conspicuous consumption post-modern society. The shirt or saree of silk is not durable, but those who wear silk shirt or saree enjoy high status in the society. More costly objects enjoy more status. The value judgement of an object is done by sign or symbol, but value judgement of status is determined by society.

Sign or Symbol

To get the consumption society attracted different kinds of symbols are used. Through symbols tempetation is created: To-day symbols is found everywhere. Objects are not sold in markets, but symbols are sold in the market now-a-day. Different type of creams, powders, lotion, soap, surf, body masssage oil, head massage oil, edible oil, etc. are not sold to-day. Rather symbols are sold and purchased. These items are sold in market with a symbol or sign of heros, heroines, beauty-queens, cricket players, Table Tennies players and so on. Even books, pencils, copies, gas stove, gas cylinder, freeze, T.V., house, car, furniture, clothes, fast food, utensils, shoes, slippers, handcker chiefs, pety cots, under wear, inner, bra are sold and purchased through symbols. The symbols has become so valuable that we kneel down before it. In fact we have become slave of symbols. The value of object lies not in utility, but in its symbols. Consumption as a symbolic system has become an integral part of post-modern culture. The system believes that symbols have regularity and it brings unity in the society. It is also believed that it is a system of morality and communication. It is a structure of exchange. This structure is above to individuals and is applicable to whole society.

Consumption was not taken into consideration in the theory of Marx. But it was included in theoretical preposition by Baudrillard. He calls consumption as social labour. He was of opinion that in early capitalism there was exploitaton of labour. In the same way, in late capitalism there is explotation of consumer. In other words labourers were exploited in modernism and consumers are exploited in post-modernism. But like Marx, he has no hope of any revolution from consumers. According to Baudrillard, consumers belong to middle class. No force can compel them for revolution. It is because consumers are related to symbols not to objects. For Marx, land, labour, capital, organisation and enterprenureship were factors of production. But for Baudrillard market is a factor of consumption. The post-modern society has a global market. Consumption society is a society where everything is for sale. Here all things are not symbols, but all symbols are things. Here every thing is exchangeable. It includes symbols, signs, services, culture, knowledge, art, literature, dance, music, beauty, sex, nakedness, vulgarity, humanbody and body parts.

Symbolic Exchange: Temptation

In simple societies, symboilic exchange is prevalent. The members of simple societies share Joys and sorrows symbolically on the occasion of birth, marriage, death, worship and festivals. They have symbolic exchange of visit, invitation, food items, food, *sacrifice, prasad, haria*, wine, clothes, ghee, curd, rice, flower, vegetable and so on. Here exchange is reciprocal and net of material objects hub of social relations. In this symbolic system things are taken and given. It is accepted and returned. It includes gifts and regifts. This exchange is non-market and non-money. It has social and cultural significance. It is not of economic significance. It is symbolic exchange which keeps members of simple society integrated. In modern society we have capitalism, but in simple society there is symbolism. In simple society production is for reciprocal exchange not for money exchange.

According to Baudrillard in post-modern society symbolic exchange has no importance, but in simple society symbolic exchange is valuable very much. In simpler society when an individual dies, symbolic tools are offered to him/her. It includes foodgrains, cooked food, milk, curd, ghee, loaf sugar, sacrifice, etc. Through symbolic exchange ancestral generation is integrated to the present generation. In market system symbols are sold, but in simpler society symbols are exchanged.

Fashion

According to Baudrillard fashion is an identity of post-modern society. Media is advertising fashion every moment. Fashions are related to dress designs, hair designs and hosue designs, car designs and ornaments design. In presenting models on T.V. services of beauty queens are hired. They wear glittering dresses, they remain half naked or they wear inner at the time of presenting fashion designs. In presenting news commercial breaks are taken in which model girls are shown in modern dresses hair styles and ornaments.

Hypermania

According to Baudrillard hypermania is an identity of post-modern society. The members of post-modern society are always found in the state of hypermania. They do not care for today nor for tomorrow. They live in an another world. They believe in eat, drink and be merry. They want to earn more and enjoy more. They do not believe in saving. It is useless to save money. They do not care for future. Thus, merchantisation and consumption have brought society in the state of hypermania.

In conclusion we can say that Jean Baudrillard was a Neo-Marxist. He in his preposition established that post-modern society of Europe is basically media society. Media has created wrong demand and it has created wrong consciousness. As a result a powerful consumption society has emerged. In this society the difference between right and wrong has been omitted. Here capitalism has incarnated in new form. In new capitalistic system, cutlure has become a thing to be sold and purchased in market. Here art, beauty, literature, sex, human body, surrogacy body organs, all are sold and purchased. Here one finds consumption culture, sale and purchase culture, lie culture, showy culture, temptation cultue, symbolic culture, simulative culture, image culture, hyper reality culture, fashion culture, hypermanic culture, hypocratic culture and so on. These cultures have become synonyms of post-modernism.

POST-MODERNISM OF JEAN FRANCOIS LYOTARD

Lyotard was a French post-modernist. He was born at Warsaleeze and educated at Perish. He was professor at an American University, Atlanta till his death. His important contributions are as follows.

- Discourse Figure 1971
- The post-modern condition: A report on knowledge 1979
- Phenomenology 1991
- Post-modern explained to children
- Towards the post-modern 1993

Lyotard has attained wider popularity through his book, *Post-Modern Condition.* He had written this book on the request of officials. He was requested to prepare a report on university education and research. Later on he got the report published in the form of the above book. One finds the description of policies related to university education and research. This book is treated as a record on university education and research. In this book Lyotard attempted to show changes brought in educational system through information technology. His another attempt was to introduce the knowledge of linguistics in other educational areas. He was of opinion that development of science and technology has taken place increasingly. The science and information technology function on the principles of linguistics now-a-day. The role of language can be seen in communication, cybernetics, mathematics, computer and data bank.

In his early life of career, Lyotard was deeply influenced by Marx. But inspite of being Marxist, he has disapproved the theory of metanarratives. On this ground he has attempted to formulate his theory of post-modernism. According to him, post-modernism is nothing, but rejection of metanarratives. His view of post-modernism was above knowledge. He was of opinion that knowledge cannot be total. Knowledge is always competitive. One knowledge comes in conflict with another knowledge. According to him, knowledge is of two types: (i) narrative and (ii) scientific. He was strong opponent of meta- narrative and totality.

The third important subject of Lyotard was related to information. He was of opinion that information is related to knowledge. In post-modern period, merchantisation of information or knowledge has taken place. Persons with more and more informations are more and more powerful. This matter is also applicable to the concept of nation-state. It is related to Advance Grade of Arts.

The main characteristics of Lyotard's post-modernism can be discussed under the following sub-headings:

- Post-modern condition
- Disapproval of metanarratives
- Metanarratives were related to industrial and commercial growth.
- Metanarratives were suffering from poor values.
- Real science is determined by philosophy.
- Modern knowledge-science is for pleasure and facilities.
- It is very difficult to formulate homogeneous society of Marx.
- Whole or parts.
- Form of fragmentation: Language game.
- Merchantisation of knowledge information.
- Expertise in technological knowledge.
- Computerisation of knowledge language.
- Utility of knowledge.
- Objectives of knowledge.
- Knowledge for sale.
- Validity of knowledge.

Post-modern Condition: In post-modern condition Lyotard has rejected the theory of metanarratives. The theories of Marx, Weber and Durkheim are called as metanarrative. Metanarratives had emerged during modern period. Due to enlightment modern society came into existence. But in post-modern period, metanarratives were not accepted. Modern society has dealt with knowledge in the context of science. Here a meaning of science is related to such a knowledge which is objective and impartial. But objective and impartial knowledge of modern period was not acceptable to Lyotard. Such types of knowledge has not been explained in metanarratives. Therefore, metanarratives cannot be accepted. This is post-modern condition, according to Lyotard.

Non-acceptance of metanarratives: According to Lyotard, theories of metanarratives are unbelievable. After enlightment the meaning of knowledge derived in society is faulty. One cannot develop faith on them. To-day knowledge has changed completely. The knowledge propounded in metanarratives is political, individual, moral, mystic and religious. It has no any valid universal theory. Its method is not applicable to whole theory. This knowledge is neither applicable to nature nor on society.

Metanarrative are related to industrial and Commercial Growth: Knowledge hidden in metanarratives have been related to industrial and commercial growth with the help of big factories, industries and automatic machines. Large scale industrialisation brought large scale production. This resulted in commercial growth. Thus, metanarratives stressed upon earning more and more wealth. They suggested that wealth earning was must for hapiness of common man. But metanarratives also increased explotation of labour along with commercial growth. Thus, exploitation had become an integral part of metanarratives.

Metanarratives suffering from low values: The metanarratives had made individual more and more selfish and important. Individuals entered in mega race of wealth earning. Individuals made themselves valueless for earning wealth. They began to earn more and more wealth through deceive, admixture and wrong means.

Philosophy determines the real science: According to Lyotard, the real knowledge can only be recognised by philosophy. Philosophy tells about knowledge, science and logic. It tells us about the final goal of science.

The knowledge of modern society for pleasure and facility: The knowledge of modern society is for more and more pleasure. Modern knowledge enhances pleasure and facilities. Men are involved in lust and passion. They want to have luxurious house, office, car, dress, food, entertainment, and journey. According to Lyotard, we should forget knowledge of modern society and we should build a post-modern society.

Impossible to build homogeneous Society of Marx: Marx had pleaded for Socialist society. But Lyotard was of opinion that it was very difficult to build socialist society everywhere. We cannot build a Socialist society by force or pressure. We can imagine about a post-modern society in place of Socialist society of Marx. Post-modern society, is an individual society and fragmented society. Now, traditional and modern society are no more. Now, we cannot imagine about whole society, but we can imagine about part or local society.

Wholeness or Partness: Lyotard was of opinion that this world is full of diversities. In this parted or fragmented world, it is useless to talk about wholeness. In this situation it seems meaningful to talk about local or parted or fragmented society. Language game, fragmentation of society, fragmentation of men present witness about fragmentation.

Form of Fragmentation*: *Language game: Lyotard has attempted to understand the relation between narratives (theory) and science on the basis of concept of language game. According to him, the work to establish the relation between narrative and science is done by language game. It is the function of language game to maintain the relation between narrartive and science. As two individuals or two societies are integrated through language game, in the same way narrative and science are integrated through language game. Without language game there will be a silence in the society and the society will be silent society. It is language games which ties the members of society.

There is no doubt that narrative and science both are form of knowledge, but both differs in their forms. This difference appears due to language game. The meaning of knowledge is taken as symbol and direction, for example how to survive, how to live, how to eat, how to behave, how to learn, how to work. This kind of knowledge is related to our traditions. For example, respect elders, love youngers, obey to elders, obey to traditions and so on. Narratives keep the members of society united through their value. Narratives gives us understanding and teach us to speak and learn. If work is performed through language game it is language games which provides integration in narratives of different regions. Thus, interactions between traditions or narratives take place through language game. Interaction in traditions or metanarratives is nothing, but language game.

Merchantisation of knowledge and Information: According to Lyotard the features of post-modern society is homogeneity, collectivity and universality. Individuality, partedness and heterogeneity are also features of post-modernity. Information and knowledge are central point of post-modernism. Industrial revolution has brought the investment of wealth in production. There is a close relation between investment and production. From the point of view of technology and knowledge, science has emerged as a power of production. Now, the aim of science is not to discover truth. Now, its aim is to bring quality and expertise in production. Through science a ratio is maintained between investment and achievements. Now, scientists are paid more salary not because they discover facts, but because they creat more quality and expertise in production. In this way, merchantisation of knowledge and information has taken place.

***Aim of technology to bring Excellence*:** According to Lyotard, the main aim of technology has been to bring excellence. Production power is hidden in technology. That is why production is brought through technology. In present day educational system special attention is being paid on technology. Now-a-day a special debate is held on quality, excellence and expertise of technology in educational institutions. Now, we do not pay attention on ideology, but we pay attention on ability.

***Computerisation of knowledge of language*:** According to Lyotard computerisation of knowledge of language has taken place. Computerised society expresses knowledge in computer language. They know language, symbols and meanings of computer language. This has brought change in the knowledge of society. This change has occurred due to computer language.

Utility of knowledge: The concept of knowledge has changed in post-modern society. Now, knowledge has been related to production efficiency. When development of technology takes place, discussion on utility of technology is started. The discussion is held on benefits which we will get from the new technology. Now-a-day, memory book, knowledge bank, e. knowledge centre, data bank and so on are taking place of a teacher. But there will be need of teacher to educate the computer language. The teacher will tell which data are relevent and which data are irrelevant. Now, discussion on technology is held in Government, students and universities.

***The aim of knowledge to make development*:** According to Lyotard, the aim of knowledge is not only for production, but also to bring progress in production. New and new technologoies are being invented. Students are being trained in new technologies. In days to come, data banks will be world dictionary.

Knowledge for sale: In traditional and modern society knowledge was for distribution. It was held that knowledge increases with distribution. But now-a-day, knowledge is for sale not to distribute or share. In post-modern society knowledge has become a thing for selling and purchasing. Now-a-day, we are involved in selling and purchasing of knowledge.

Validity of Knowledge: According to Lyotard knowledge is found in both metanarratives and science. But their validities are different. The knowledge in metanarratives is based on myths and traditions. But knowledge of science is based on evidence. Knowledge is key of modern society: That is why it is based on truth.

POST-MODERNISM OF JACQUES DERRIDA

Derrida was born in Algeria in 1930. He was educated from a famous educational institute of Peris named Nichole Normades. He was a follower of jew religion. In 1965 his two important essays were published in Research Journal named critic. After publication of these essays he was established as a French Scholar. His essays were related to Grammar. Now, he was recognised as linguist. He was known as post-structuralist. The important contributions of Jacques Derrida are as follows:

- Speech, phenomena and other essays 1973
- Of Gramatology 1967
- Writing and difference 1967
- Positions 1972
- Disseminations 1972
- Margins of Philosophy 1972
- Glass 1972
- The Truth in Paintings

Derrida was influenced by philosophers like Loke, Berkley, Home. Being influenced by these philosopher, Derrida had started talking about deconstruction in the context of language and epistemology.

Derrida's Concepts of Deconstruction

A number of definition has been provided to modernism. According to one definition post-modernism is a movement which is visible philosophy, art, architecture, literature, poetry, dance, drama, films etc. From an another definition post-modernism is a mentality. This mentality is not against modernism. It is related to reconstruciton of modernism. Post-modernism presents modernism in a different perspective and meaning.

The post-structuralism of Derrida is based on deconstructions and discrimination. According to him, deconstruction is a philosophy. This philosophy has reached to literature, education, art, psycho-analysis and social theory from philosophy.

The concept of deconstruction is related to language. Through concept attempt has been made to understand the importance of language in social relationship of man. A man is a man. He has a self. He is also a memebr of the society. In between self, man and society, the work to establish relationship is done by language. An individual acquiers knowledge about self, man and society through language.

Thus, inbuilding self in man language and society play significant role. Like a society, a self is developed in individual. The developer or promotor of self is language. Language is related to text. Some meanings used in a text are quite clear, but some meanings are not clear. In this situation the first task of deconstruction is to highlight the clear meanings of unclear meanings of a text. In other words we can say that deconstruction is nothing but to clarify the meanings of unclear meanings of a text. The deconstruciton philosophy highlights the weaknesses of a text. Thus, language makes the scheme of philosobhy a complex. All are equal in deconstruction philosophy. Criticism, philosophy, linguistics and anthropology all are deconstruction objects for Derrida.

The concept of deconstruction is based on logic of deconstruction. There are two meanings of discrimination. First meaning is related to discrimination. The second menaing is related to disapproval. In this way, we can say that critical study of text is deconstruction.

Explaining language, Derride has attempted to distinguish between speech and writing. Speech is speaking form of language and writing is graphic form of language. One maintain his memory power through writing. We can achieve past information and knowledge through study of writing form of language. But in language the speech occupies first position. Writing has second place in language. Speech is related to phonology. It is deeply connected to our ideas. Therefore, speech is primary and basic. Our writing is secondary. It has no origionality. It has artificiality and ornamentation. This distinction between speaking and writing can also be applied in social areas. Deconstruciton is a means to know the meaning of terms used oral or written. It is such a method in which meanings are taken out by connecting one terms with another terms. In this method words are not added to event. The individuals who describes the events are indicators. The language and terms which he uses have different meanings. The complete or truth meaning is always unclear. Truth also has different meanings. The meaning of language cannot be searched in a concrete reality. It can be searched in the context of language self. It has social context. It is created socially. Through the philosophy of deconstruction so called truth is rejected. If there is an imagination in text, it must he rejected. It is because imagination cannot be truth.

Derrida was a Grammarian: He has taken the help of text in his philosophy of deconstruction. As the text of grammar is above the author, similarly the text of language is also above the writer. The meaning which author has in mind is changed by reaching to readers. All these appear as a game of terms. The meaning of text is individual and subjective. It is not objective. The same term has different meaning and different terms have same meaning. Terms have their own social context.

If we study the text of *Vedas*, we come to know that wherever women are worshiped, deities reside there. This attaches high value to women in vedic society. When we study text of *Ramayana*, we find women subjected to refinment like drum, rustic and shudras. When we compare the values of women in both texts, we do not find what is truth about woman. To discover this truth is known as deconstruction philosophy.

We can also find out a deconstruciton philosophy from an another example. In our sacred texts husbands have been regarded as *Parmeshwar* (Great God). But prostitute visiting husbands, drunkard husbands and dishonest husbands have been treated as beast. On comparing the two context, we do not understand what is truth about husbands. They are great God or great beast. The husband may be in the category of God or in the category of beast. This may be truth. It means that husbands are not objective, rather they are subjective. An individual may be a God or a beast as a husband.

POST-MODERNISM OF FREDRIC JAMESON

Philosopher like Fukuyama had established the end of history in 1989 in his book, '*The End of History*' in which he opined that now there was no chance to emerge the Socialist society. Now, the imagination of a classless and stateless society was just an imagination. But Marxist and post-modernist writer Jameson had explained capitalism in a new way. All post-modernists had disapproved the metanarrative, but Jameson accepted the metanarrative of Marx, but in a modified form. He termed his new theory as *late capitalism*. He opined that in post-modern society the development of capitalism is not taking place through labour, rather it is taking place through cultural activities. Marx had treated culture as super structure. He had isolated culture from capitalism. But modern capitalism is stressing upon becoming richer and richer with the support of culture. In this way Jameson provided a new cultural logic to capitalism. He presented Marxism in a new form. In fact, he revitalised the Marxism. He opined that the economy of today made the culture a thing of sale and purchase. Like other things, culture is being produced. Today we have social pluralism and cultural pluralism. To-day we have many kinds of people with many kinds of cultures. To-day there is no class system. But we have local groups in present day. We have now political group, regional group, artists groups, art lover group, etc. In absence of class, movements are taking place in place of conflict. In this way, Jameson provided a new thought to Marxism. His important contributions are as follows:

- ***Political unconscious***: Narrative is socially symbolic Act 1981.
- Post-modernism are the cultural logic of late capitalism 1991.
- ***Geopolitical Asthetic:*** Cinema and space in world system 1992.
- The seeds of time 1994.

Jameson had attempted to understand post-modernism as a cultural logic of late capitalism. According to him, capitalism has assumed different forms in different periods. Marxist capitalism is a capitalism of vast production. Then corporate capitalism came in to existence. Now-a-day, we have late capitalism. Late capitalism is one of features of post-modernism. The emergence of late capitalism has made a thing to be sold and purchased. Culture was regarded as auspious heritage transmitted from one generation to the next honestly. But late capitalism and post-modernism have made culture a commodity which can be sold and purchased anywhere in the market. In post-modernism commodification of culture has taken place.

Developmental Stages of Capitalism

Jameson did not agree with the views of Daniel Bells who had opined that now we were living in post-industrial stage. But Jameson was not ready to accept it. He was of view that we were living today in late capitalism. Like late industrialism, there was also a stage of late capitalism. He has talked about three developmental stages of capitalism which are as follows:

- ***Market Capitalism*:** This stage of development of capitalism was from 1700 to 1850. In this age industrial revolution had taken place. The development of industrial capitalism had taken place in this period. As a result, markets were developed. Industrial capitalism in its initial stage was concentrated on national market.
- ***International Market*:** When production in national market was increased in nineteenth century the needs of big markets were felt. As a result international market came into existence. Now, capitalism reached in international market. East India company came for trade in our country. French traders is also came for trade. They also reached to Africa. But in the competition of trade. East India company got a chance to establish imperialism and colonialism. In the capitalism of India and Africa, there was dominance of market. This capitalism had not touched our culture. Colonialist economy

gave many advantages to imperialist market. It provided cheap labour, raw material and customers.
- ***Monopoly Market*:** This market is a modified form of international market. This market is based on late capitalism which came into existence in 1990. In this decade several social and economic institutions emerged which began to present culture in new forms. The culture got its astonishing significance in market, temple and chruch. New deities were discovered. Vanished traditions were revived. Disappeared festivals appeared again. State and politcal power also extended their support in incarnation of culture in new form. The joint effort of all these commodification of culture took place. Now, culture was not for culture, but for market. Similarly, art, architecture, entertainment, literature all were now for market.

In this way Jameson established the concept of late capitalism. He attempted to understand it on the basis of commodification and marketisation. Now, we are living in the stage of late capitalism. Now, we have culture to sell and purchase in market. Now, dance, music, song, literature, entertainment, art, beauty all are being sold in markets. In the act of selling and purchasing, artists, literaturists, dramatists, singers, musicians, religious leaders and Government are involved. They are extending full support to sale and purchase of culture.

POST-MODERNISM OF ANTHONY GIDDENS

Anthony Giddens was a British Social Anthropologist. He was born in 1938. He had received his education from Hell University, London. He did Ph.D. from London School of Economics. He was also director of London School of Economics. His educational life may be divided in to two parts. The first part of life is between 1970-1980. In this period of his career he developed the concept of structuration. The second part of his career begins from the middle of 1980 decade. In this period he developed the concept of post-modernism. His important contributions were as follows:

- The Constitution of Society: Outline of the theory of structuration 1984.

- Profiles and critics in Social Theory, 1982.

Structuration Theory

While formulating his theory of structuration Giddens criticised the existing theories whole heartedly. He disapproved the theories of Marxism, functionalism, structuralism, symbolism and interactionism. His aim behind formulation of structuration theory was not different from other theoreticians. Like other theoreticians he was interested in discovering truth.

His theory of structuration is a theory of school ontology. Through this theory he wanted to know as to what things were happening in the world and which factors were contributing in development of those things. Giddens was not interested in finding out solution of these questions. His interest was also not in mobility of things. According to him, the social structure and action of individual cannot be isolated. Individual builds social structure and social structure influences individual. Individual not only can builds social structure, but he can disorganise structure and rebuild social structure. In this sense, social structure is not an external object. It is product of individual. Individual builds social structure through his behaviour. Structure is not satic, rather it is dynamic concept. It is a continuous process.

Criticism of different theories: As mentioned earlier, Giddens have criticised all earlier theories. His criticism of different theories are being given below.

Disapproval of Naturalism and Positivism

Giddens had disapproved the theory of naturalism and positivism because he did not consider social science as natural science. According to him the nature of social science is quite different from the nature of natural science and positivism. While criticising naturalism and positivism he has paid attention on three things:

- People are themselves theoreticians of social structure.
- Like natural science no timeless theory can be propounded in social science.

- Social theory is not an outside object of society.

***Solution of Sociological Dualism*:** According to Giddens there are several dualism in sociological theory. They need to be solved. Due to dualism ontological analysis has to face problems. Some dualisms are as follows:

- Micro *versus* macro
- Subjective *versus* objective
- Individual *versus* society
- Material *versus* ideal

Due to above dualism we do not understand the society completely.

The above dualism are not in isolation. They are complementary to each other. They are interdependent and interrelated. They maintain their co-existence.

***Criticism of Functionalism and Evolutionism*:** According to Giddens evolutional theory came into existence in nineteenth century and functional theory came into existence in twentieth century, but these both theories are irrelevent now-a-days. According to functionalism in order to fulfil the needs of man, structure is always in its existence. According to evolutionism, evolution of society goes on continuously to reach in the stage of modernity. Both functionalism and evolutionism see society in the same way. But, both these theories are useful to understand the society. Marxism has also nourished evolutionism. Therefore, its utililty is also doubtful.

***Criticism of Interactionism*:** Giddens was not only critic of evolultionism, Marxism, functionalism and positivism. Rather he was a critic of interactionism, too. According to him, interactionism supports dualism. This theory does not tell us as to why interactionism rebuilds the structure. Institutional processes also bring change in structure. For example untouchability (prohibition) Act 1955 has brought major change in the traditional status of *Dalit* in our society. This change is real in pen and paper. In interactionism, feeling has no importance. Interactionism provides importance to role. But social activities bring a change in entire society. Ban on sale of wine and tobacco by Panchayat has brought a real change in economic and social status of rural family. Interactionism has not included such social process in its theory.

***Criticism of Structuralism*:** Giddens was also critical of structural theory of Levi-Strauss. According to him the theory of structuralism is fully dependent on linguism. Levi-Strauss has never accepted that boundary of social structure is built by the ability and efficiency of the people. The structural theory has failed to understand this fact that social structure is always changed by the interaction of active people. It is also redefined.

GIDDENS THEORY OF STRUCTURATION

After disapproving evolutionism, Marxism, functionalism, structuralism and interactionism, Gidden has propounded the theory of structuration in his book, *Constitution of Society* (1984). According to him, structuration theory is alternative to all earlier theories. He was of opinion that all sociological theories may be placed under two groups. In one group, those thinkers have been included who treat structure as a system, and deny the importance of individual or subject. According to these theoreticians individuals have no separate existence. Structuralism Marxism and functionalism come under the first group. Another group of theoreticians hold view that society is built as a result of integration of individual and his/her activities. Therefore, without individuals the system has no existence. Without individual and his activities structure cannot be formed.

According to Giddens in Sociological theories there is clarity of individual and structure as dualism. Therefore, attempt should be made to get rid of this dualism. We can get freedom from this dualism through the theory of structuration. We should move forward taking individual and structure together. We should view them not in isolation, but as a complement to each other. He was against dualism, but not against duality. Individual utilizes the available structure, but he also utilises alternatives available in structure.

The basic elements of structuration are rules and sub-rules. At the time of interaction, the individual or subject obeys rules and sub-rules. Thus, rules are method of interaction. For example when we meet elders, relatives, friends, teachers, we offer *Pranam*. This is one of rules of interaction. The structure makes this rule valid.

Individuals externally know the meaning of this. This rules, according to Giddens has following characteristics:

- Rules are used in work
- Its use takes place in interaction
- These rules are obeyed in daily life
- These rules are unwritten and informal
- The pressure of these rules is low.

The individual or subject knows all these characteristics. Giddens have attempted to define institution as interaction. Institutions, infact, are interactions found in society. Marriage, family, kinship, caste, class etc. are not for one or two days. Their life span is lengthy. According to Giddens institutions are of four types:

- Discourse of symbol, language and communication
- Political institutions
- Economic institutions
- Legal institutions.

According to Giddens, structure and institutions are two chief traits of structuration. Individual and structure are two main poles of structuration. He calls individuals as agent in technical word. The individual who takes part in social actions are termed as agent. Agents pay special attention on social practice in social actions. At all places structure and restructure of social practice takes place. Agents know about it. Agents have applied knowledge. He travels in same train and in same class in same coach of which he/she buys a journey ticket. This shows practical knowledge of agent. The agents known the rules and regulations of society. The agents have discursive consciousness, too. He/she knows well that if caught without ticket journey, he/she will have to pay penalty fixed by T.T.I. The agents also have third kind of practice which is known as unconscious practice. This practice is due to fear and pressure. This develops discipline in agents. In this way, structuration of our society has taken place from social practice.

According to Giddens, action is a process of structuration. Each action has a knowledge. Each action has some meaning esstentially.

10
Industrialism and Post-Industrialism

Introduction

The school of anthropological thought which deals with the theory of industrialism and post-industrialism is known as industrialism school and post-industrialism school. According to this school industrialism has been a characteristic of modernity. Other characteristics of modernism were democracy and military power. But industrialism was a central power. In the middle of twentieth century industrialism was at peak. Thereafter, a revolutionary change took place in economy. This economic change created such a situation due to which post-modernism came into existence. The economy of modernism was capitalist. In this period mega industries were established in Europe. The main purpose of this economy was mass production. When we imagine about an industrial society, we see smoke coming from big factories, air pollution, water pollution, sound pollution, slums, labour and labour movement. Mass production gave rise to two major problems which were as follows:

- Problem of raw material
- Problem of market

These two problems gave rise to imperialism. Now, industrialism was changed in such a way that colonialism got entrance in Asia and Africa and imperialism came there. This brought a new turn in economy. Now, production was not mass production, but fragmented production came into existence. Transportation, communication and fragmentation made society decentralised. Now demands for different things came. As a result mass production was changed into flexible production. Liking of common people was changed completely change in liking brought change in production. In industrial society emphasis was placed on mass production, in post-modern society emphasis was given on flexible production. The place of modern industrial society has been taken by post-industrial society. The post-industrial society has gradually assumed the form of post-modern society. The post-modern society is not only post-industrial society, but also has elements like communication system and new ideology.

In post-industrial society emphasis is placed not on production of things, but on services of things. This has brought an increase in knowledge and information related to production. It means that in making industrial society to a post-industrial society, the role of information technology is of great importance. Now-a-day such technologies have emerged in which we have to employ less labour and obtain more production. Now, work of a labourer is done by machine. Labour, now, control the machine. In fact, the work of production is done by machine. New economy has been established in industries which is known as knowledge economy. This has created a new society known as post-industrial society and knowledge economy society.

Knowledge economy is such an economy in which different forms of knowledge, idea and information play significant role in economic growth. In knowledge economy labourers do not have to render labour physically. They have not to distribute things. They have to make only designs of things. They have to develop technology related to those designs. They have to pay attention on advertisement, communication and marketing. Such workers are now, known as knowledge workers. Now, they do not render their physical labour, but now they render their knowledge with the help of technology. Now, they are not labourers of production economy, but they are knowledge workers of information or knowledge of economy. Here technological development and innovation go on continuously.

In knowledge economy such things are not produced which can be stored, loaded and unloaded at different places. In this economy service, information and advice are provided. This has given birth to grand trade.

Thus, we see that complete transformation of work in post-industrial society has taken place. Previously things were produced in large scale. Things had standard value. They were known by same name all over the world. Now, we have a number of markets and a number of likings. This forced the producers to give-up orthodox behaviour and to adopt flexible behaviour in production. Their production has become flexible. In this way transformation of work has taken place. Post-industrial society, thus, has knowledge economy and knowledge workers. This society achieves economic growth with the help of knowledge, information and technology. Knowledge and information help in innovation. Innovation is key of knowledge economy.

In post-industrial society think work came into existence in place of physical work. This has brought knowledge elite in existence. Knowledge elites provide their services in different areas. The concept of knowledge elite has divided post-industrial society into elite worker and unemployed. Elite workers get handsome packages, while majority of people being unemployed are forced to work on less payment. Elite class enjoys all kinds of pleasures, while unemployed class is forced to work as domestic workers at very low payment or nominal payment. This has made commoditisation of domestic work. Thus, post-industrial society is a divided society.

In post-industrial society production is flexible. When women started driving cars in Europe and America, cars were produced in such a way that they were more suited to women in driving. Now, production is done on the basis of speciality. Before production, demands are taken into consideration.

There is lack of division of labour in post-industrial society. Here emphasis is placed on team work. Here production is done by team work. Team members get their goal fulfilled with their team work. They work day and night to save their skill and interest.

In post-industrial society we find multi-expertise. Here the same worker does not perform the same work till his retirement. Rather he/she is expected to perform different works. Workers with multiple expertise are preferred by the employer. In this way, the worker of post-modern society is a multi-expertise individual.

From the above presented account, the following characteristics of post-industrial society may be hightlighted:

- Knowledge economy
- Flexible production
- Knowledge workers
- Knowledge elite
- Think work
- Team work
- Team production
- Multi-expertise
- Divided society
- Information society

11
Globalisation

Introduction

Globalisation may be defined as a process of integration by which different countries of the globe have become interdependent and interrelated socially, culturally, economically, politically and environmentally. This process emerged invisibly in mid-1980s decade and visibly in 1990s decade. Thus, process is 25 to 30 years old. But during this short span, globalisation has influenced not only all countries of the world, but also scholars belonging to different disciplines. All nations of the globe have accepted it as a model of development and moving forward with the help of science, information and technology. Scholars of different disciplines of different nations of the globe have recognised the importance of information technology in gaining more and more knowledge from scholars situated apart and diffusing own knowledge to scholars resided in different parts of the globe. Now, the technology of study and research has also changed. Computer, internet and overhead projector have become aid of the need of day for study, teaching and research. But inspite of all these benefits of space technology, the process of globalisation has divided the scholars of the globe in two groups—one group supports the globalisation and the other group opposes the globalisation. Those scholars who support the globalisation consider it essential for the development—social, cultural, educational, environmental, health, economic and communicational. But those who opposes the globalisation treat it anti-development of various kind. Both groups of schoars have their logic behind supporting and opposing the globalisation process. But they are more critical of Americanisation, unemployment, low payment, temporary appointment and exploitation caused by the globalisation. Even critics have recognised the significance of space technology.

The scholars have attempted to look at the porcess of globalisation from the point of view of their own discipline. For historians, globalisation is a historical process. The historical process of globalisation started after the dissolution of USSR in 1989. Now, America became the global power. The world became from bipolar to unipolar so far as power was concerned. The American Scholar Francis Fukuyama wrote his famous book, *The End of History* (1989). In this book Fukuyama has attempted to deal with the end of history of mankind. According to him, now, nothing more than capitalism, democracy and secularism are going to occur in the history of mankind. Thus, the history of mankind has come to an end and the process of globalisaiton interms of capitalism, democracy and secularism has started.

For sociologists, the process of globalisation has created a global village society. The members of this society have digital and space technology through which they maintain their interrelationships and fulfil their various kinds of need. For the members of this global village society time and distance are not a trouble in communication.

For economists, globalisation is a model of economic development. This model is being used as a means for the development of economic growth by almost all nations of the glob.

For political scientists, the process of globalisation has decreased the power of nation-state and has brought the concept of global governance and e-governance.

For natural and biological scientists, the process of globalisation has brought a revollution in information technology.

For anthropologists the process of globalisation has resulted in knowledge revolution in the history of mankind. According to anthropologists, four major revolutions have taken place in the history of mankind till now. They are as follows:

Major Revolution	*Related Process*	*Period of beginning*	*Form of Society*	*For of economy*
1. Agricultural	Peasantisation	Neolithic	Peasant	Agricultural
2. Urban	Urbanisation	Bronze age	Urban	Non-agricultural
3. Industrial	Industrialisation	19th Century	Industrial	Industrial
4. Knowledge	Globalisation	1990	Global village society	Knowledge economy

For literaturists, the process of globalisation has brought the concept of deconstruction and dualism in texts. It reveals the truth mentioned in texts.

From above description, it is clear that scholars of different disciplines have attempted to understand the globalisation from the point of view of their own disciplines. But it is true that the people of local and global have become interdependent and interrelated through digital technology and space technology in the era of globalisation. The invention of W.W.W. has redefined the concept of time and place. This discovery has connected all people of the globe all time through digital and space technology.

Liberalisation, Privatisation and Globalisation (LPG) are closely related, and inter-dependent. They maintain their co-existence. One cannot imagine about globalisation without liberalisation and privatisation.

The originator of globalisation process is regarded as Silicon Valley of California in U.S.A. It is because of this fact that globalisation is criticised as Americanization. But infact globalisation process is not an Americanisation process. This process has compelled all Governments of the globe to introduce the process of liberalisation and privatization in order to facilitate globalisation process. The liberal policies of the Government of different nations of the globe have opened the scope for private multinational companies to flourish everywhere. Multinational companies are not only Americans, but they are British, German, Japanese, Chinese and even Indian. Multinational companies have emerged due to liberalisation and privatisation. It is because of this fact liberalisations, privatisation and globalisation are uttered together.

Theme of Globalisation

From the above accounts of globalisation, it is clear that different schoars have conceived globalisaiton differently. Some scholars treat it only as an economic concept. Some other treat it as a social and cultural concept, while still some others treat it as political, health and environmental concept. Besides these of general opinions of scholars, let us consider some special opinions of scholars on globalisation.

According to Anthony Giddens globalisaiton is result of modernity. The globalisation process has influenced the time and distance in social life in a new way. He has termed it as time-space distancination. In this way, according to him, increasing reciprocality, interdependence and interrelatedness in different areas of the globe is globalisation. Giddens has expressed this views in his book, *Consequences of Modernity* (1991).

An another theoretician of globalisation Harwe De in his book, *The Condition of Post Modernity* (1989) has added the concept of historicity in the concept of time-space distancination of Giddens. According to him, time and distance not always maintain continuity. They have not been same historically. In recent years there has been tremendous growth in capitalism. The main reason was disorganisation of USSR. After disorganisation of USSR, the time and space have changed. A new global system has been established in the world. This system has provided a new direction to time and space. Therefore, the distancination of time and space should be seen in historical perspective.

Wallerstein Imamuel in his book, *Historical Capitalism* (1991) has defined globalisaiton as a result of capitalism. He was of opinion that for distancination of time and space in globalisation process, global capitalist economy was responsible.

Regenauld in his book, *Turbulance in World Politics* (1991) has defined globalisaiton process as a world-wide communicaiton system through information, digital and satellite technology. According to him, globalisation is such a process which has created distancination of time and space through latest technological advancement. The reciprocity, interrelatedness and interdependence found in world today are due to digital and satellite technological system. Through the medium of digital and satellite technologies, local, national and International communities have become integrated and a special kind of relationship has been established.

R. Gilpin in his book, *Political Economy of International Relations* (1989) has defined globalisation as a product of political factors. According to him, globalisation is a political process through which powerful nations entrust their economy and culture on developing nations. In this way they establish their economic and cultural globalisaiton on the people of developing nations.

According to International Sociological Conference (1998), the social sciences have accepted globalisation in place of universalisation. But globalisation is plural in its meaning. Now, diversities have entered in the global village society.

According to European Commission, globalisation is such a process by which markets and products of different countries have become more and more interdependent reciprocally. Although social and cultural factors are involved in it, but the basic nature of globalisation is economic.

Melcom Waters in his book, *Globalisation* (1998) has attempted to show that in the globalisation there is sufficient inclusion of local and global processes. There is no geographical and national boundary in the process of globalisation.

Characteristics of Globalisation

From the opinions and definitions provided by different scholars, the following characteristics of globalisation can be noted:

- Globalisation have come into existence in 1980s invisibly and in 1990s visibly.
- It has created the concept of time and space distancination.
- It is product of capitalism.
- It is product of digital and satellite technologies.
- It has made all people and nations interdependent and inter-related reciprocally.
- It has placed special emphasis on liberalisation, privatisation and investment.
- It has integrated the local and global processes.
- It has created a new form of global society.
- It has given birth to a new form of global culture.
- It is a system of digital and space technologies.
- It is related to knowledge and information revolution.
- It has made knowledge a global powerful force.
- It has created new technologies.
- It has new global markets.
- It has new agents and organisations W.T.O. IPR, NGOs etc.
- It is governed by new rules and regulations.

- It is a political process.
- It has omitted geographical and national boundaries.

Some Dualism Associated with Globalisation

The process of globalisation has created some dual terms. It is fitness of the thing to deal with those dual terms one-by-one. The main duality created by globalisation are as follows:

- Local *vs.* global
- Tradition *vs.* modernity
- Universalisation *vs.* specification
- Humanism *vs.* discrimination
- Integration *vs.* disintegration
- Centralisation *vs.* decentralisation
- Affinity *vs.* fear
- Individuals *vs.* society
- Self *vs.* others
- Ideal *vs.* real
- Real *vs.* hyper real
- Market *vs.* service
- Truth *vs.* untruth
- Objective *vs.* subjective.

Local vs. Global: It is true that the process of globalisation has created a global society and culture. But it is also true that it has made us aware of numerous local societies and cultures through televisions and internet. Thus, both local and global cultures are going side-by-side. But it is also true that the process of globalisation has created local and global duality.

Tradition vs. ***Modernity***: It is true that globalisation has made us aware of global modern fast food culture, dress culture, and modern pop culture. But is also true that it has highlighted the traditions of the people of the globe about which we were not knowing. In the era of globalisation the people have been attracted towards modernity, but they have also recognised the value of their traditions. Local people are also launching movements to revive their lost traditions, while some are continuing their traditions in revived form. Thus, tradition and modernity both have attracted the people and both are persisting side-by-side. But the duality of tradition *vs.* modernity have come into existence in the era of globalisation.

Universalisation vs. ***Specification***: The process of globalisation has created the duality of universalisation *vs.* specification. If it true that globalisation has universalised the restaurant and fast food culture all over the globe, but it has also attached significance to the local specific food value. The universal fast foods are being modified and specified according to local needs. For example vegetarian, non-vegetarian, sugar free, salt free, garlic free, onion free foods. In this way globalisation has created the duality of universalisation *vs.* specification.

Humanism vs. ***Discrimination***: Globalisation has provided equal opportunity to all ethnic groups to adopt urban and metropolis life style, Jobs in I.T. sectors, management sectors, multinational companies, travel in A.C. cars, trains, plains, staying in five star hotels, travel trip to foreign countries, job opportunities in foreign countries, modern houses with facilities, visit to costly restaurants and entertainment centres. The process of globalisaiton has made available such life style above ethnic groups. In this way it has promoted humanism. But the process of globalisation has also created discrimination. It has divided human beings into rich and poor in all ethnic groups. In all ethnic groups some are rich, while others are poor. It has created a big gap between rich and poor in all ethnic groups. In this way globalisation has created the duality of humanism and discrimination.

Integration vs. ***Disintegration***: The process of globalisation has created the duality of integration *vs.* disintegration. Undoubtedly globalisation has integrated the people of the globe socially, culturally, economically, educationally, politically, and environmentally through information technology. But it has also created disintegration. For example it has disintegrated the labour organisations. The followers of same religion are disintegrated at local level.

Centralisation vs. ***Decentralisation***: The process of globalisation has created the duality of centralization *vs.* decentralisation. Undoubtedly, America has emerged as a central power. It has sufficient power, wealth and storage of information. In this way power is centralised in the hand of America. But it has also created decentralisation. Local people are agitating for solution of their local problems.

Affinity vs. ***Fear***: The process of globalisation has created the duality of affinity *vs*. fear. There is no doubt that the process of globalisation has brought affinity among people maintained by redefining the concept of time and space. It has brought similarity in work style of people of the globe. But local people are always fearful that they will lose their tradition and culture. Thus, in globalisation one finds affinity and fear both.

Individual vs. ***Society***: The process of globalisaiton has created the duality of individual *vs*. society. The globalisation has freed the individual from the bondage of society. Now, he or she is not expected to follow norms and values. He or she is expected to lead a life according to own will not as per the will of society. He or she is free to lead a life of eat, drink and be merry. He or she is free to lead a married life or unmarried life or live in relationship. He or she may reproduce young ones or adopt a child born from surrogacy. But for majority of local people society is essential for collective living. In this way globalisation has created the duality of individual *vs*. society.

Self vs. ***Others***: The process of globalisation has created the duality of self *vs*. others. The globalisation has created the self-centred individuals. It has made individual selfish. Even husband, wife and children care for only self not for other members of the family. Each member of family has become competitive. He or she remains busy in own work and promotion. He or she has money, but not time to share feelings with other members of the family. But on the other hand, the globalisation has also brought such people to light who are always ready to help others.

Ideal vs. ***Real***: The process of globalisation has brought the duality of ideal *vs*. real. In several sacred texts one finds description about ideal culture. But in practice ideal is not real. In sacred texts we find women as Goddess and husbands as lord or God. But in practice neither women are goddess nor husbands are lord. The globalisation has presented before us both the duality.

Real vs. ***Hyper real***: The globalisaiton has brought the duality of real *vs*. hyper real. In televisions we are shown varieties of advertisements with the help of beauty queens. But those advertisements are not real they are hyper real. It is because we take them as true and consume them without knowing the reality. But the truth comes out after consumption. Then we have only to repent. Thus, the globalisation has brought the duality of real *vs*. hyper real.

Market vs. ***Service***: The globalisation has brought to the light the duality of market *vs*. service. The globalisation has brought such an international market which remains operative 24 hours. It has made everything marketable. It means that everything, sale and purchase. Art, culture, entertainment objects, dance, beauty, food, creativity, books, poems, songs, beauty and so on are for sale and purchase. In this way globalisation brought marketisation of everything. But it has also developed the concept of service. Now, we have different kinds of service providers who are ready to serve us anywhere and anytime on the payment of charges. Thus, globalisation has created the duality of market *vs*. service.

Truth vs. ***Untruth***: The process of globalisation has brought before us the duality of truth *vs*. untruth. With the help of latest space information technology it brings before us the truth or untruth related to an event, phenomenon, behaviour, practice and knowledge which are taking place in the world. In this way, globalisation has created the duality of truth *vs*. untruth.

Objective vs. ***Subjective***: The process of globalisation has created before us the duality of objective *vs*. subjective. It has brought before us both kinds of knowledge subjective and objective.

Types of Globalisation: Keeping impact of globalisation on social, cultural, economic, political, health and environmental life of people of the globe, globalisation may be of following types:

- Social globalisation
- Cultural globalisation
- Economic globalisation
- Political globalisation
- Health and environmental globalisation

Social globalisation: The process of globalisation has created the concept of global village society. The members of this society maintain their social relationship with the help of digital space information technology. Now-a-day some new terms have been innovated for the society. They are as follows:

- Global village society
- Information society
- Media society
- Consumption society
- Computer society
- Knowledge society
- Internet society
- Cellphone society
- Space society
- Digital society
- Satellite society
- Google society
- U tube society
- Digital society
- Chating society
- Dating society
- Post-modern society
- Electronic society
- e-mail society

These terminologies have been innovated to deal with society with the help of new satellite digital information technology.

Cultural globalisation: The process of globalisation has created similar types of culture all over the globe. New terms have been innovated to deal with culture. They are as follows:

- Global culture
- Shared culture
- Media culture
- Information culture
- Consuming culture
- Computer culture
- Internet culture
- Cellphone culture
- Space culture
- Satellite culture
- Digital culture
- Chating culture
- Dating culture

- Electronic culture
- e-mail culture
- Google culture
- U tube culture
- Advertising culture
- Restaurant culture
- Fast food culture
- Pop culture
- On line mate selection culture
- On line marriage culture
- On line divorce culture
- On line worship culture
- On line inauguration culture
- On line death ritual culture
- Surrogacy culture
- Live in relationship culture
- Same sex marriage culture
- Tourism culture
- Hospitality culture
- Plural culture
- Drawing room culture
- Nursing home culture
- Old age home culture
- Play school culture
- Beauty contest culture
- Marketing culture
- Entertainment culture
- Cultural corporation
- Cultural traders
- Cultural globalisation of ethnicity
- Ethnic market culture
- Corporate culture
- Knowledge culture
- Global welfare culture
- Disaster management culture

Economic Globalisation: The process of globalisation has created the concept of economic globalisation through space digital technology. It includes multinational companies, multinational workers, multinational trade and multinational market. In order to show the process of globalisation, the following new terminologies have been innovated:

- Multinational enterprises
- Corporate enterprises
- Corporate industrialisation
- Corporate economy
- Knowledge economy
- Knowledge workers
- Knowledge trade
- Knowledge market
- International market
- World trade organisation
- World as shopping complex
- International Division of Labour
- On line marketing
- ATM and Debit card facility
- On line payment
- On line delivery
- Globalisation of financial markets
- Migrant labour
- Globalisation of classes producers, consumers and distributors.
- Globalised economy
- Intellectual property right
- Liberalisation
- Privatisation
- Off shooting and off shoring
- In sector
- Management sector
- Business communication
- Temporary appointment and low payment
- World Bank and International Monetary Fund.

Criticism of Economic Globalisation: The main criticism against economic globalisation are as follows:

- The process of globalisation has enhanced the process of privatisation, liberalisation and intellectual property rights.
- Illegal trades of illegal arms have increased in this era.
- Terrorism has become a global problem.
- The disease of AIDs has spread in all countries from Africa.
- International environmental problem has become a global problem.
- The gap between rich and poor has widened.
- The exploitation of children in third world countries has increased.
- The exploitation of women in third world countries have gone up.
- Local markets are terrified from global markets.
- Cottage industries have been omitted.

Political globalisation: The process of globalisation has integrated the countries of the globe politically. In order to show political globalisation, the following phrases have to be innovated:

- Decline in nation-state power and influence.
- No control of state on markets
- The attachment of sovereignity with greater organisation
- Origin of global rule
- Emergence of Human Rights
- Protection of global environment
- Joint cooperation during disaster
- New political culture—capitalism, democracy and secularism

Decline in Nation-state power and influence: With the help of liberalisation and privatisation, the globalisation process has been able to decline the power and influence of nation-state. Now, any member of any nation or state can initiate his/her business entrepreneurship in any state or nation. Such entrepreneurs are known as multinational entrepreneurs or multinational company. They have their intellectual property rights and are controlled not by the Government of a state or nation. Rather they are controlled by world trade organisations. Thus, nation-state now, has no control over economic policies and markets. Now, the policies of a nation or state is influenced by globalisation and the power of nation-state has declined.

Decline in traditional rights of state: Defence, communication, and economic system come under the traditional right of a state. But the process of globalisation has declined the influence of state on these traditional rights. The influence of global political institutions have increased on the traditional rights of a state.

Attachment of state sovereignty with greater organisation: Sovereignty is a feature of a state. The state does not tolerate the encroachment of another state in its territory and rights. But due to the process of globalisation the Sovereignty of a nation is attached to greater international organisation. The state has to make compromise with international organisations. For example, NATO, OPEC (organisation of petroleum exporting countries), UNO, IMP etc.

Emergence of Global Rule: Due to the process of globalisation, global or international rule has come into existence. The rights and boundaries of states have become narrowed. Now, we have international army to fight collectively against terrorism, violation of human rights and disarmament. America has established his army stations in a number of countries of the world. Joint army of several countries has been posted at several places.

Emergence of Human Rights: Due to the process of globalisation, now, the human right has emerged as a global problem. Now all countries, have started steps to guarantee human rights to children, women, aged, S.Ts. S.Cs. OBCs and other deprived, exploited and oppressed lots and to make them empowered. Now, we have International Human Rights Commission, National Human Rights Commission and State Human Rights Commission.

Protection of Global Environment: Due to the process of globalisation, the nations of the state have started special drive to protect and preserve the environment. The importance of environment has been recognised globally and due steps have been initiated to conserve them and protect environment. It is because man cannot survive without healthy environment. The environment is not only for few nations and individuals. Rather, it is for all people of all nations and for generations to come. Therefore, to protect the race of man, protection of environment is a must. We are living now in a risk society which is full of pollution risk and we are bound to suffer from a number of diseases. Now, all nations have joined their hands to preserve and protect the environment globally.

Emergence of Joint Cooperation during Disaster: The process of globalisation has given birth to joint cooperation among countries of the world during natural disasters like flood, earthquakes, Tsunami, Storms, starvation and so on. Now disaster is not a national problem but a global problem. All countries of the globe extend cooperation to the victim country to come out of the tragedy and handle problem carefully and scientifically.

Together fight against AIDS: Due to the process of globalisation all countries of the globe have extended full support to fight against the AIDS. All countries have launched programmes to make people aware of the disease of AIDS protection from it and its treatment.

New Political Culture: The process of globalisation has given a new political culture to the nations of the world. This new political culture is of liberal capitalism, democracy and secularism. There is, now, no alternative of this political culture of the world. In the period between 1975 and 1997, the number of democratic states has become double. Even the Islamic theocratic countries are adopting the elements of democracy. Today all nations are united to save humanity during flood, earthquakes, epidemics and AIDs. This new global political culture is outcome of democracy.

Resistance to Globalisation: It is true that globalisation has been adopted by all nations as a model of development. But it is also true that society is not static, rather it is dynamic. The society has passed through several fast changes. First of all enlightment came into existence. Then modernism came and then society reached in post-modern state. Along with post-modernism globalisation came into existence. Due to globalisation all nations of the globe become interdependent and interrelated reciprocally. But it is also true that globalisation is basically a capitalist process. This process protects the interest of capitalist nations and multinational corporations. The globalisation has omitted the existence of a number of nation-states. Multinational corporations have huge investors. They are controlling the entire globe. These people have pushed the entire people of the globe in ditch of pollution. They are spreading AIDs and sexuality. The people of the globe have become aware of risk created by process of globalisation. The people of developing countries have started raising their voices against globalisation in organised manner. Resistances have appeared in economic, social, cultural, political and environmental areas of the globalisation.

Today globalisation has made the globe a shopping complex. Multinational corporations control the global production technique, financial capital and market. They make study of local culture first and then produce things according to uses of that culture. In this way globalisation has created a new kind of economic and cultural imperialism. Some scholars call it as media imperialism. Or it has created consumption society.

It is also true that all nation-states have not adopted the process of globalisation. Some nation-states have moved backward in economy due to globalisation. Their cottage industries have been closed. The gap between rich and poor has increased. The problem of unemployment has increased. The exploitation of women, children and labour has increased. Local markets have been abandoned. Rural artisans have become unemployed.

Technological system occupies prime place of importance in globalisation. But all countries do not have equal knowledge and means of technological system. They are not in a situation to invest. Local markets have gone out of control from their hands. It is because of this reasons that backward nations and states resist the process of globalisation.

Mobilisation against Globalisation

It is true that nation-states have adopted globalisation as a model of economic development. But it is also true that the process of globalisation has to face mobilisation. In the world after cold war, equality and social justice had become a theme of distant for different nation-states. The gap between rich and poor nation-states went on increasing. The unemployment and poverty witnessed tremendous increase. Increasing unemployment proved that marketism is not solution of all problems. A need of alternative was felt. The civil society was taken as an alternative of globalisation and marketisation. It was felt that the civil society should press the nation-state to remove the gap between rich and poor.

In connection to civil society as an alternative and its role in omitting the gap between rich and poor, two great conferences were held in Europe in 2001. One conference was held in Bonn of Germany and the other conference was organised in Geneva of Italy. These two conferences sent a clear messages to the world that poor nations would not close their mouth and sit idle against global capitalism. In Bonn conference 178 countries had participated. In Geneva Conference G7 countries had taken part. America, Britain, Canada, France, Germany, Italy and Japan had taken part in it.

These two conferences discussed, in detail, on risk of pollution created by mass production. Rich nations are responsible for environmental pollution. They are enthrusting different kinds of diseases on the people of poor nation-states. In Geneva Conference 1.25 lacs of people stood against the globalisation.

Criticism: Some of criticisms against globalisation are as follows:

- Globalisation has put human life under risk.
- Globalisation has created new technology, but it has made. many nation-states backward.
- Poor nation-states are not feeling safe due to it.
- It has made many youth unemployed.
- It has created temporary appointment and low payment.
- All nation-states do not have sufficient wealth for computer, internet and cell phones.
- It is beneficial for wealthy nations.
- 80 per cent languages websites are run in English language.
- It lacks websites in local languages.
- It has divided the world into rich and poor.

12
Karl Marx's Legacy in Anthropology

Introduction

It is fitness of the thing to present here the theory of Karl Marx or Marxism in the interest of the readers because entire anthropological theory has revolved round materialism *vs.* idealism or a synthesis of materialism and idealism.

Middle classes of Europe had prospered in the wake of French revolution. The prosperity of middle classes of Europe had made the working classes restless and agitated for reform. When industrial revolution had taken place in Britain, radical intellectuals had rallied to support the growing labour movement. The most radicle support had come from Karl Marx and Friedrich Engels, the co-creators of theory of dialectical materialism. Dialectical materialism is commonly called as Marxism because it is philosophy of Karl Marx and Friedrich Engels. Marxism had influenced the real world of politics profoundally. Marxism had also influenced anthropology not only for this reason, but also because aspects of Marx's thought were elaborated and formally incorporated within anthropological theory even by anthropologists who in no sense were Marxist in their allegiance.

Contribution of Karl Marx

Karl Marx (1818-1883) was born in Prussia. He had studied philosophy at University of Berlin and then law at the University of Bonn. He had became interested in the relationship between politics and economics, turning to Utopian variety of socialism in 1843. Early he had decided that Utopian socialism was ineffective and to become effective socialism would have to be made scientific.

Friedrich Engels (1820-1895) was a son of German Textile manufacturer who had spent several years in English cities of Manchester and Liverpool as the agent of textile firm. England had already experienced the undesirable effects of industrialisation and was debating parliamentary measures to improve the poor conditions of Urban workers. Engels analysed these conditions in his book, *The Condition of Working Class in England* (1844). Then he expanded his analysis in collaboration with Marx. The result was their landmark treaty, *The Communist Manifesto* 1848.

The essential ingredients of dialectical materialism can be found in the Communist Manifesto and the much larger work *Das Capital* (1867). Marx and Engels began with the premise of materialism, meaning their belief that human existence determines human consciousness. Their concept of materialism was contrasted to the concept of idealism, the belief that human consciousness determines human existence. Marx and Engels believed that human thoughts, actions and institutions are determined by their relationship to the means of production, meaning how people make a living in material world. This relationship is always changing, because the means of production are always changing as people change their adaptations to physical conditions. From contemporary anthropology Marx and Engels drew their analysis that in prehistory people lived in a socio-economic system with material goods belonging to all, no private property and equality under the law. In civilization powerful individuals gained control of land, the basic source of wealth. Thus, primitive communism was superseded by a system of all equal classes and exploitation of one class by another.

Marx and Engels maintained that all modern societies are based on class distinctions. These distinctions become institutionalized in church and state which keep the ruling class, the class that controls the means of production, in power. As the means of production change, the nature of classes, which organise the means of production also changes. Eventually, the means of production outgrow their form of organisation, which is overthrown in social revolution, from which a new social system emerges. In classical Marxism, the sequence of social revolutions is dialectical, according to a revised version of philosophy of George Wilhelm Friedrich Hegel (1770-1831). Hegel was an extreme idealist. He had described a world spirit manifesting itself in history through dialectical transformations of forms-thesis-antithesis-synthesis. The thesis came first, followed by its opposite, the antithesis and then followed by a combination of the thesis and antithesis, the synthesis. Marx and Engels were attracted towards Hegel's philosophy. But they felt that it needed to be up-ended epistemologically. Therefore, they stood Hegel on his head and moved the dialectic from the ideal to the material world. In the resulting theory dialectic materialism, social transformations assume a dialectical form. With one social stage the thesis, sowing the seeds of its own destruction by harbouring its opposite, the second stage anti-thesis, which manifests itself in social revolution. This stage is followed by a third social stage, the synthesis that retains elements of the proceeding two stages-thesis and antithesis. The main focus of Marx and Engels was materialism than dialectics. Their primary interest in revising Hegels theory was to use it to explain what had happened in world history and what would happen in future through a communist revolution.

Marx and Engels were aware of prehistory, ancient history, and non-western history, but they had begum their account with the middle ages and feudalism. In feudalism, a system of agricultural economics, there were two classes. They were the ruling class lord and the ruled class serf-unfree labourers. But during feudalism a new manufacturing class had also come into existence. The power of capitalists in feudalism rested on money rather than on land. The capitalist means of production was manufacturing and superior to agriculture and eventually replaced it. For Marx and Engels, the triumph of capitalism over feudalism was French revolution. After French revolution lords and serfs were superfluous. The new ruling class bourgeoisie (middle class) and ruled class proletariate (urban workers) had come into existence.

Marx and Engels were not interested in spending time for the analysis of feudalism and how it gave rise to capitalism. But they were much more conscious to analyse, capitalism and how it would give rise to communism. Their analysis was based on labour theory of value. It was the materialist premise that goods and services should be valued interms of the human labour required to produce them.

According to this theory the value of good or service, a commodity, is directly related to the amount of labour put into it. Exploitation occurs when capitalists expropriate some of these value as profit. Moreover, capitalist buy and sell labour itself as a commodity, valuing it according to wages determined by labour market. The result is that workers are alienated from product of their labour and therefore, from themselves.

The main focus of Das Capital was disintegration of capitalism. In this book Marx explained that capitalism was progressive in the beginning and had opened up new markets as an efficient way of producing goods. But capitalism became regressive later on. It become less efficient as competition between manufacturers decreased and economic power was concentrated in fewer and fewer hands. The growth of monopolies was inevitable. Competition produces gainers and losers both. Ultimately monopoly system outgrew the original capitalist system of product diversity. Rich monopolists got richer by increasing profit and poor workers became poorer because profit was taken from their wages. Proletariat became pauperised and small business people were squeezed out by competition. This swelled its ranks. Under free market conditions, a glout of labourers caused a decease in wages intensifying poverty. Due to cheaper labour profits increased. Profits were reinvested in production for a while, but production generated more and more goods able to be bought by fewer and fewer people. This downward spiral of events led to economic recession, depression and labour unrest. Soon the capitalist world was ripe for revolution.

In the mature phase of capitalism, the means of production would be concentrated in few locations. Workers could easily size them in the name of proletariat and nationalize them in the name of nation governed by workers. The first stage of revolution would be temporary dictatorship of the preliterate, whose job would be to destroy bourgeoisie as a class and eliminate private profit by putting it to public uses. The result would be classless society in which church and state, formerly serving the interests of few capitalists, would become an agent of all workers. Eventually, the state would wither away and the final stage would emerge. The final stage would be true communism. In this stage workers would work according to their ability and receive compensation according to their needs. Final communism would represent a return to primitive communism with the technology of industrial age.

Marxism achieved major political victory in Soviet and Chinese revolutions of twentieth century. These revolutions led to the installation of Marxist dogma and its modification by powerful politicians Lenin, Stalin and Mao Tse-Tung. Marxism also took root outside politics in academic discipline like anthropology.

In 1930s, a small minority of anthropologists professed allegiance to one or more of tenets of Marxism. Marxist anthropologists are diversed. But except for structural Marxists of 1970s and later, most of them stand on common intellectual ground. Few of them accept the entire theory of dialectical materialism, which history has helped refute. But they do demonstrate a personal commitment to help oppressed and disadvantaged group and are willing to use anthropology professionally. Theoretically, they prefer materialist in place of idealist. In cultural analysis they emphasize class because Marxism implies that different classes have different ideologies and consciousness, often fundamentally opposed. In Marxist circles there are disputes between vulgar materialists and Marxist anthropologists. The vulgar materialists are simple minded materialists. Marxists anthropologists who embrace one form or another of dialectics. They are also known as structural Marxists who blend classical Marxism with twentieth century anthropology of French structuralist Claude Levi-Strauss. They have criticised positivist anthropologists who promote value free science.

13
Max Weber's Legacy in Anthropology

Introduction

As Max Weber has influenced the writing of twentieth century anthropology, political economy and post-modernism, it will be the fitness of the thing to present here the contributions of Max Weber.

French sociologist Emile Durkheim had used the concept of organic solidarity to understand integration among social groups. German scholar Karl Marx had understood human history as an engine to pull physical conditions of forward. Both these scholars were of view that forces which are active outside individuals, create cultural meaning and structure of social relation, according to their own will. These outside forces are socio-psychological at one hand and dialectical on the other hand. In the theories propounded by Durkheim and Karl Marx, there was no place for creative agency or individuals. Both had shown subjects of their theories as homogeneous idle. For this they were also criticized. They had treated individuals as mindless and continuous obeyers of those active forces which control all aspects of existence.

Contrary to his counterparts Marx and Durkheim, the German scholar Max Weber treated individuals as active for creation, obeyance and innovation of social and cultural forms. Because of this reason Max Weber is regarded as idealist and scientists. The idealism of Max Weber was quite different from the materialism of Karl Marx. But this concept is also confusing because no known society has creative agency as a basis of relation between production and reproduction. But it is also true that Weber has presented a synthesis of idealism and materialism very effectively.

Contributions of Max Weber

- Protestant ethics and spirit of capitalism 1920
- The Sociology of Religion (1922)

Weber was interested in knowing as to how the development of society has taken place in course of time. That is why he is known as an evolutionist. But his view on evolution was not unilineal like nineteenth century classical evolutionist. He had presented existing beliefs and structures in his theoretical scheme of evolution. That is why he is identified as a multilineal evolutionist. His theory of evolution presents a great diversity of human life.

The evolutionary scheme of Max Weber can be presented in the following manner.

The complex society has originated due to progressive specialization and intensification of labour. Due to progressive specification and intensification of labour several layers of class emerged of social and economic nature. As a social and historical environment move towards complexity, physical inequality of these classes also moves towards complexity. The inequality between privileged ruling class and military class and non-privileged artisan class and trader class became more and more complex. The artisans and trader classes were deprived of social and political power. They become conscious towards economic marginalisation. Due to difference between experience and hope towards world (what is and what should be) theodicy developed. Weber discussed the concept of theodicy within the religious framework. Weber had taken the concept of theodicy from Christian sacred Text (Bible). He discussed the concept of bad or harmful on the basis of theodicy. According to him like God bad or harmful is also universal.

According to Weber, religion is an engine of pulling forward social change with time. The despair of merchant class and their alienation from power foster deep anxieties about the apparent senselessness of the world. If one lives according to the wishes of a good and powerful deity fulfilling all ritual observances and prescribed behaviour, then why the world is so problematic. This dilemma raised a voice for resolution. Weber saw the resolution of this dilemma in salvation For his formulation of social change Weber believes that salvation is achieved through the radical restructuring of beliefs about the world. This prescribes ethical behaviours to bring people into accord with this new vision.

Inner worldly asceticism is the central disposition involved in this process. This process entails removing oneself from corrupt worldly indulgences, while remaining within the world of human activity paradoxically. For Weber, inner worldly asceticism opposed to outer worldly ascetics-monks, hermits etc., who seek literally to escape the social world and its influence by retreating to special spaces (monasteries deserts) where worldly things have no power or authority. By refraining from indulgence in specific corruption which is here in the world, inner worldly ascetic remains virtuous even while participating in other non-corrupting aspects of worldly life. (Judeo-Christian standard). Crucially for Western society, material prosperity is not only excluded from this catalogue of iniquity, but becomes a hallmarks of one's standing *vis-à-vis* divine will. The stimulus for such reformulation and renewal is understood to have come from especially creative individuals, charismatic prophets. Charismatic prophets claim to receive a new revealation of divine truth that will reintegrate belief and action. In doing so charismatic prophets claim to restore psychosocial harmony to humanity.

The most significant example of an embodiment to this process came from Calvinist Protestantism. It is a diverse body of Christian doctrine and practice whose origins are traced to the teaching of John Calvin, oppositing Roman Catholic Claims to authority and believing in a Christianity based on verbal inspiration of scripture and justification of faith. Calvinist Protestantism is a religion of urban merchant which rationalized a new relationship between human beings and God. In this way a French theologian John Calvin (1509-1564) was considered as a prophet bearing a new vision of human life. Under this new Covenant revealed to Calvin, individuals were directed to create heaven on earth through hard work as prescribed by God in scripture and obedience to divine will. Middle class professionals were elevated to a position of ethical superiority in this models. They were no longer dominated by ruling elites. Now, Urban merchants and artisans began to view themselves as a community of believers united to certain ethical tenets, the adherence to which would definitely lead to a more rewarding materially and satisfying life emotionally. The merchant look at their material prosperity as a sign of God's grace. The burgeoning culture of sixteenth century renaissance commerce linked in this way to cosmological order become an increasing by compelling blue print for action in world. In people behaved in a certain way prescribed by God, they would be rewarded materially here and spiritually justified in hereafter. This new system of meaning and action ultimately resulted in the global triumph of industrial capitalism.

The anthropologists of recent generations have recognised the significance of Weber's social evolution theory. In recent years the discipline of anthropology has become more concerned with issues pertaining to the creative agency or individuals, the cultural worlds they construct and inhabit and various permutations of consensus and conflict that exists within and between cultures.

The most prominent personality who adopted Weber's thought in anthropological analysis explicitly was Anthony P.C. Wallace. In his influential historical ethnography about Iroquois, *The Death and Rebirth of Seneca* (1972), Wallace applied the concept of revitalization movement, which was fully formulated in his theoretical work, *Religion: An Anthropological View* (1966). In above both his work, Wallace has drawn heavily on Weber's idea that during periods of cultural crisis Charismatic prophet rationalises a new and a more satisfying religious worldview for members of a society.

A second classic Weberian study is Peter Worsley's *The Trumpet Shall Sound* (1968). Here Worsley has shown that many indigenous people of Indonesia and new Guinea are led by variety of charismatic prophets in a series of millennial cargo cults. The studies of Worsley and Wallace are strikingly similar that both have examined socio-cultural contexts in which colonial powers place severe economic, political and cultural stress on the colonised people generating a breakdown in the indigenous social order. In both settings revitalizing social movements rationalise the impact of colonialism into world views that stipulate the omnipotence of a super natural power or agent who will ultimately restore harmony and happiness if specific ethical and behavioural criteria are adhered to.

Jean and John Comar off's book, *Of Revealation and Revolution*, has analysed the impact of colonialism in South Africa applying many of same concepts. In the light of these and similar analyses, which highlight the transformative potential of human agency, Weber's synthesis of materialism and idealism has seemed in some ways more useful. Marx's theory which is often viewed as reducing culture to an effect of material concern.

7
Bibliography

Anderson, Benedict, (1991): *Imagined Communities: Reflections on the Origin and Spread of Nationalism*. London: Versa.

Archihold, W. Peter (1992): Marx and the Missing link. *Human Nature: Atlantic Highlands*, New Jersey: Humanities Press International.

Ardrey, Robert. (1961): African Genesis: A Personal Investigation into *Animal Origins and Nature of Man*, New York: Antheneum.

Banister, Robert C. (1988): *Social Darwinism: Science and Myth*, Philadelphia: Temple University Press.

Barton, Michael (1988): *Racial Theories*. Cambridge: Cambridge University Press.

Barret, Stanley R. (1996): *Anthropology: A Students Guide to Theory and Method*. Toronto: University of Toronto Press.

Benedict Ruth (1989) [1934]: *Pattern of Culture*. Boston: Houghton, Mafflin.

Berger Peter L. and Thomas Luck Mann (1967): *The Social Construction of Reality: A Treaty in Sociology of Knowledge*. New York: Double day.

Berlin, Iaiah (1996): *Karl Marx: His Life and Environment*.

Binford, Lewis R. (1983): *In Present of the Past*. London: Thames & Had Son.

Boas Georgch (1966): *Essays, Primitivism and Related Ideas in Middle Ages*, New York, Octagon Press.

Bohann, Paul and Markglazer (Ed.) (1989): *High Points in Anthropology* 2nd ed.

Boon, James A. (1972): *From Symbolism to Structuralism: Levi-Strauss in Literary Tradition*. New York: Harper & Raw.

Burdieu, Pierre (1977): *Outline of a Theory of Practice*. New York: Cambridge University Press.

Bowler, Peter J. (1986): *Theories of Human Evolution: A Century of Debate*, Baltimore: Johns Hopkins University Press.

Bowler, Peter J. (1989): *Evalution: History of an Idea*. Berkley: University of California Press.

Bowler Peter J. (1989): *The Mendelian Revolution: Emergence of Hereditarian Concepts in Modern Science and Society*, Baltimore: John Hopkins University Press.

Bowler, Peter J. (1996): *Charles Darwin: Man and His Influence*, New York: Cambridge University Press.

Caffrey, Margaret M. (1989): *Ruth Benedict of Stranger in this Land.*

Camaroff, Jean, and John L. Camarof (1991): *Of Revealation and Revolution*. Chicago: Chicago University Press.

Carroll, J.B. (Ed.) (1996): *Language, Thought and Reality*: Selected writings of Benjamin Leewhort. New York: John Wiley & Sons.

Cassidy, Roheart (1982): *Margaret Mead: A Voice for the Century*, New York: University Books.

Chanipagne, Ronald (1987): *Claude Levi-Strauss*. Paris: Belfond.

Chaste, Elenor H. (Ed.) (1994): *Culture and Human Development*: The selected papers of John Whiting, New York: Cambridge University Press.

Classen, Cheryl (Ed.) (1994): *Women in Archaeology*, Philodelphia: University of Pennsylvania Press.

Clifford, James (1988): *The Predicament of Culture, 20th Century Ethnography Literature and Art*. Cambridge, Massachusetts: Harvard University Press.

Clifford, James, and George E. Marcus. (Eds.) (1986): *Writing Culture: Poetics and Politics of Ethnography*.

D'Andrade, Roy (1955): *Development of Cognitive Anthropology*, New York: Cambridge University Press.

Dalnel, Regna (1990): Edward Sapir: *Linguist, Anthropologist and Humanist*. Berkley: University of California Press.

Daniel, Glyn E. (Ed.) (1981): *Towards a History of Archaeology*, New York: Thomes & Hudson.

Daniel, Glyn E. and Colin Renfrew (1988): *The Idea of Prehistory*, Edenburg: Edenburg University.

Darwin, Charles (1964) [1859]: *On the Origin of Species: A Facsimile* of First Edition, Cambridge, Massachusetts: Harvard University Press.

Darwin, Charles (1981) [1871]: *Descent of Man and Selection in Relation to Sex*. Princeton: New Jersy.

Dawkins, Richard (1989) [1976]: *The Selfish Gene*, 2nd ed., New York: Oxford University Press.

Dirks, Nicholas, B., Geoff Eley and Sharry B. Ortner (Eds.) (1993): *Culture/Power/History: A Reader in Contemporary Social Theory*, Princeton, New Jersey: Princeton University Press.

Doughals, Marry (1980): *Edward Evance Pritchard*, New York: Viking Press.

Durkheim, Emile (1966) [1897]: *Suicide*. New York: Free Press.

Durkheim, Emile (1982) [1895]: *The Rules of Sociological Method*, New York: Free Press.

Durkheim, Emile. (1984) [1893]: *The Division of Labour in Society,* WD Hall, Trans., New York: The Free Press.

Durkheim, Emite. (1995) [1912]: *Elementary Forms of Religions Life*. Karen E. Fields, Trans. New York: Free Press.

Engels, Friedrich (1972) [1884]: *Origin of Family, Private Property and State*, 2nd ed., New York: International Publisher Company.

Ericson, Paul, and Liam D. Murphy (1998): *History of Anthropological Theory*, Broad View Press.

Fabion, Johannes (1983): *Time and Other: How Anthropology Makes its Object*, New York: Columbia University Press.

Fortes, Mayer. (1970): *Kinship and Social Order: The Legacy of Lewis Henry Morgan*. Chicago: Aldine.

Foucault, Michael (1982): *Archaeology of Knowledge*, New York: Pantheon Book.

Fried, Merton H. (1967): *The Evolution of Political Society: An Evolutionary View*. New York: McGraw Hills Company.

Gacs Ute *et al.* (Eds.) (1988): *Woman Anthropologists: A Biographical Dictionary*.

Gramsci, Antonio (1992): *Prison's Note Book*, Vol. I. New York: Columbia University Press.

Gramsci, Antonio (1996): *Prison's Note Book*, Vol. II. New York: Columbia University Press.

Greenand B.O. (1987): *The Birth of Prehistoric Chronology: Dating Methods and Dating System in 19th Century Scandinavian Archaeology*, Bradford, on Avon: Moonrakar Press.

Green, Selly (1981): *Prehistorian: A Biography of V. Gordon Chille*. Bralford, On Avon: Moonreffer Press.

Greek, Clifford. (1976) [1973]: *Interpretation of Culture*. New York: Basic Books.

Greetz, Clifford. (1996): *After the Fact, Two Countries, Four Decades, One Anthropologist*, Cambridge, Massachuesetts: Harvard University Press.

Gross Kurth, Phins (1988): *Margaret Mead: A Life*, London: Penguin.

Hall, Robert A. (1987): *Leonard Bloom Field: Essay on His Life and Work*. Philladelplia: John Benjamin's, North America.

Harris, Marvin (1968): *The Rise of Anthropological Theory*.

Harris, Marvin (1979): *Cultural Materialism: The Struggle for a Science of Culture*, New York: Random House.

Harris, David R. (Ed.) (1994): *The Archaeology of V. Gordon Childe*. Concord, Massachuesetts: Paul & Company, Publisher Consortium.

Henalff, Marcal (1991): *Claude Levi-Strauss*, Paris: Beltond.

Henary, John (1997): *The Scientific Revolution and the Origin of Modern Science*, Old Tappan, New Jersey: MacMillan.

Herskovits, Mellville, J. (1953) *Franz Boas*, New York: Sirebnagar.

Hobs Bawm, Erric J. and Terence Ranger (Eds.) (1992): *Inventions of Traditions*, New York: Cambridge University Press.

Holder Ian (1986): *Reading the Past: Current Approaches to Interpretation in Archaeology.*

Honlingman, John J. (1975): *Development of Anthropological Ideas,* Michigan: Books on Demand.

Hull, David. (1990): *Science as Process: An Evolutionary Account of Social and Conceptual Development of Science*, Chicago: Chicago University Press.

Hymes, Dell (1983): *Essays in History of Linguistic Anthropology*, Philadelphia: John Benjamin's, North America.

Hymes, Dell (ed.) (1974): *Studies in History of Linguistics: Traditions and Paradigm*. Ann Alor, Michigan: Books on Demands.

Jinkins, Alam (1979): *The Social Theory of Claude Levi-Strauss*, London: MacMillan.

Jones, Robert A. (1986): *The Sociological Theory of Emile Durkheim Thousand Oaks*, California: Sage Publications.

Kardiner, Abram and Edward Preble (1961): *They Studied Man*, Cleaveland, Ohio: World Publishing Company.

Klukhohn, Clyde (1961): *Anthropology and Classics*, Michigan: Books on Demand.

Kohn, Thomas S. (1970): *The Structure of Scientific Revolution*, 2nd ed., Chicago: University of Chicago Press.

Kroeber, Alfred, and Clyde Klukhohn: *Culture: A Critical Review of Concepts and Definitions*, Cambridges, Massachuesetts: Peabody Museum of American Archaeology and Ethnology.

Larson, Edward J. (1996): *Sex, Race and Science*, Baltimore: Johns Hopkins University Press.

Leach, Edmand R. (1989): *Claude Levi-Strauss*, Chicago: Chicago University Press.

Lett, James (1987): *The Human Enterprise: A Critical Introduction to Anthropological Theory*, Colorado: West View Press.

Lewin, Harry (1969) : *The Myth of Golden Age in Renaessance*, Bloomington: Indiana University Press.

Levi-Strauss, Claude (1974) [1949]: *Elementary Structure of Kinship*, James Herbell *et al.* (ed.), Boston: Beacon Press.

Levi-Strauss, Claude (1974) [1963]: *Structural Anthropology*, New York: Basic Book.

Loke, John (1994): *Essay Concerning Human Understanding*, New York: Promothus Books.

Lowie, Robert H. (1960) [1920]: *Primitive Society*, London: Roupledge and Kegan Paul.

Lutz, Catherine (1988): *Unnatural Emotions: Everyday Sentiments on a Micronesian Attol and their Challenge to Western Theory*, Chicago: Chicago University Press.

Lyotard, Jean Francois (1984): *The Postmodern Condition*, Manchester: Manchester University Press.

Maasen, Sabine (1995): *Biology as Society and Society as Biology*, Norwell, Massachuesets: Kluwer Academic Publishers.

McNairn, Barbara (1980): *The Method and Theory of V. Gordon Childe.* Edinburg: Edinburg University Press.

Magnarella, Paul J. (1993): *Human Materialism*, Florida: Florida University Press.

Mali Joseph (1992): *Rehabilitation of Myth*, New York: Cambridge University Press.

Malinowski, Brownislaw Kasper (1989) [1967]: *A Diary in Strict Sense of Terms*, California: Standford University Press.

Marcel, Mauss (1990) [1924]: *Gift: The Form and Reason for Exchange in Archaic Societies*, New York: W.W. Norton.

Marx, Karl and Friedrich Engels (1992) [1848]: *Communist Manifesto*, New York: Oxford University Press.

Mayer, Ernst (1990): *The Growth of Biological Thought: Diversity, Evolution and Inheritance*, Massachuesetts: Belk Hop Press of Harvard University.

Minz, Sideny W. (1986): *Sweetness and Power: The Place of Sugar in Modern History*, New York: Penguins Books.

Moore, Jerry D. (1997): *Vision of Culture: An Introduction to Anthropological Theories and Theorists.*

Morgan, Lewis Henry (1985) [1877]: *Ancient Society*, Tucson: University of Arizona Press.

Morris, Desmond (1980): *The Naked Ape*, New York: Dell Publishing Company.

Murphy, Robert Francis (1972): *Robert H. Lowie*, New York: Columbia University Press.

Ned, James V. (1994): *Physician to Genepool: Genetic Lessons and Other Essays*, New York: John Wiley & Sons.

Netting, Robert M.C.M. (1977): *Cultural Ecology*, Massachuesetts: Cummings Publishing Company.

Parkin, Frank (1992): *Durkheim*, Oxford University Press.

Radcliffe Brown, A.R. (1964) [1922]: *The Andaman Islanders*, New York: Free Press.

Radcliffe-Brown, A.R. (1965) [1952]: *Structure and Function in Primitive Society*, New York: The Free Press.

Rappaport, Roy A. (1968): *Pigs for Ancestors: Ritual in the Ecology of New Guinia People*, New Heaven: Yale University Press.

Redfield, Robert (1971) [1956]: *Peasant Society and Culture: Anthropological Approach to Civilization.*

Roseberry, William (1989): *Anthropologies and Histories: Essays in Culture, History and Political Economy*, New Brunswick, New Jersey: Rulgers University Press.

Rosenau, Pauline Marie (1992): *Post-Modernism and Social Sciences,* Princeton: Princeton University Press.

Ruse, Michael (1984): *Sociobiology: Sense of Non-sense*, Rev. ed., Norwell, Massachuesetts: Kulwer Academic Publisher.

Saidi, Nadar (1992): *The Birth of Social Theory: Social thought in Enlightment and Romanticism,* Maryland: University Press of America.

Sahlins, Marshal D. (1976): *The Use and Abuse of Sociobiology: An Anthropological Critique of Sociobiology,* Ann Aboor: University of Michigan Press.

Sahlins, Marshal D. (1987): *Islands of History*, Chicago: Chicago University Press.

Sahlins, Marshal D., and Elman R. Service (Eds.) (1960): *Evolution and Culture*, Ann Aboor: University of Michigan Press.

Sanderson, Stephen H. (1992): *Social Evolutionism: A Critical History.* Cambridge, Massachuesetts: Black Well.

Sapir, Edward (1958): *Culture, Language and Personality: Selected Essays David Mandel Baum* (ed.) Berkley: University of California Press.

Schneider, Peter and Jane Schneider (1986): *Culture and Political Economy in Western Society*, Orlando, Florida: Academic Press.

Service, Elman R. (1962): *Primitive Social Organisation: An Evolutionary Perspective*, New York: Random House.

Service, Elman R. (1985): *A Century of Controversy*, Orlando, Florida: Academic Press.

Seymour, Smith Charlbotte (1986): *Dictionary of Anthropology*, Boston: G.K. Hall & Company.

Spiegelberg, Herbert (1982): *Phenomenological Movement: A Historical Introduction* (3rd ed.), The Hang: Martinus.

Steward, Julian H. (1972) [1955]: *Theory of Culture Change: Methodology of Multilinear Evolutionism,* Campaign: University of Illinois Press.

Stocking, George W. Jr. (1982): *Race, Culture and Evolution: Essays in the History of Anthropology*, Chicago: University of Chicago Press.

Stocking, George W. Jr. (ed.) (1990): *Bones, Bodies and Behaviour: Essays on Biological Anthropology*, Madison: University of Winsconsin Press.

Stocking, George W. Jr. (1994): *Collected Works of E.B. Tylor*, New York: Routledge.

Stocking, George W. Jr. (1985): *Observers Observe: Essays on Ethnographic Fieldwork*, Madison: University of Winsconsin Press.

Stocking George W. Jr. (1992): *The Ethnographers Magic and other Essays in the History of Anthropology*, Madison: University of Winsconsin Press.

Stocking, George W. Jr. (1984): *Functionalism Historicised: Essays on British Social Anthropology* (1880-1951), Madison: University of Winsconsin Press.

Strenaski, Ivan (1992): *Malinowski and the Work of Myth*, New Jersey: Princeton University Press.

Trigger, Bruce G. (1980): *V. Gordon Childe: Revolutions in Archaeology,* New York: Columbia University Press.

Trigger, Bruce G. (1990): *A History of Archaeological Thought*, New York: Cambridge University, Press.

Turner, Victor (1967): *Forest of Symbols: Aspects of Ndembu Ritual*, Ithaca, New York: Cornell University Press.

Tuner Victor (1969): *The Ritual Process: Structure and Antistructure*, Howthorne, New York: Aldienede, Grayter.

Tylor, Stephen (1969): *Cognitive Anthropology*, New York: Holt, Rinehart and Winston.

Tylor, Edward Burnett (1871): *Primitive Culture*, New York: Grandson Press.

Tylor, Edward Burnett (1881): *Anthropology: An Introduction to the Study of Man and Civilization*. New York: D. Appleton.

Van, Gennep Arnold (1959): *The Rites of Passage*. Chicago: Chicago University Press.

Vermeulean, Han, and Artural A.R. Rolds (Ed.) (1960): *Fields Works and Foot Notes: Study in History of European Anthropology*. New York: Routledge.

Voget, Fred W. (1975): *A History of Ethnology*, New York: Holt, Riveheart and Winston.

Wallace, Anthony F. (1966): *Religion: An Anthropological View*, New York. Random House.

Wallace, Anthony F. (1972): The Death and Rebirth of Seneca, New York: Random House.

Wallerstein, Immanuel (1974): *The Modern World System: Capitalist Agriculture and the Origin of World Economy in Sixteenth Century,* Orlando, Florida: Academic Press.

Weber, Max (1996) [1920]: *The Protestant Ethic and Spirit of Capitalism,* Los Angeles: Roxbury.

Weber, Max (1993) [1922]: *The Sociology of Religion*, Bostom: Beacon Press.

Whiter, Leslie A. (1949): *The Science of Culture*, New York: Grave Press.

White, Leslie A. (1959): *The Evolution of Culture: The Development of Civilization to the Fall of Rome*, New York: McGraw Hill.

Wilson, Edward O. (1975): *Sociobiology: The New Synthesis*, Cambridge, Massachuesetts, Belknap Press of Harvard University.

Winthrof, Robert H. (1991): *Dictionary of Concept in Cultural Anthropology*, New York: Green Wood Press.

Index